Florida

The Acts and Resolutions adopted by the General Asssembly

of Florida

Florida

The Acts and Resolutions adopted by the General Asssembly of Florida

ISBN/EAN: 9783337170684

Printed in Europe, USA, Canada, Australia, Japan

Cover: Foto ©ninafisch / pixelio.de

More available books at **www.hansebooks.com**

THE

ACTS AND RESOLUTIONS

ADOPTED BY THE

GENERAL ASSEMBLY OF FLORIDA,

AT ITS

TWELFTH SESSION,

BEGUN AND HELD AT THE CAPITOL, IN THE CITY OF TALLA-
HASSEE, ON MONDAY, NOVEMBER 16TH, 1863.

———•◦•———

PUBLISHED BY AUTHORITY OF LAW,
UNDER THE DIRECTION OF THE ATTORNEY GENERAL.

———•◦•———

Tallahassee:

OFFICE OF THE FLORIDIAN & JOURNAL.

PRINTED BY DYKE & SPARHAWK.

1863.

TITLES

OF

ACTS AND RESOLUTIONS

PASSED AT THE

Second Session of the Twelfth General Assembly

OF THE

STATE OF FLORIDA,
1863.

An act to repeal an act entitled an act to regulate trade and intercourse with the Indians.

An act authorizing publication to be made out of the State of sales by Administrators and Executors in certain cases.

An act to change the place of holding the Circuit Court for Putnam County.

An act to amend Ordinance No. 53 of the Convention in relation to soldiers voting.

An act for the protection of cattle owners in the counties of Levy, Lafayette Taylor, Wakulla and Duval.

An act amending the Charter of the City of Pensacola.

An act for the relief of James W. Johnson of Taylor county.

An act to change the line dividing the counties of Suwannee and Columbia.

An act to amend the Charter of the City of Pensacola, so as to authorize said City to aid in the construction of certain Railroads.

An act to incorporate the Apalachicola Channel Company.

An act to be entitled an act to allow the Judges of the Circuit Courts of this State to appoint Sheriffs in certain cases.

An act to amend the sixth section of an act entitled an act to change the mode of selecting Grand and Petit Jurors in this State, approved February 8, 1861.

An act to legalize entries of public lands made after the secession of Florida and requiring the Receivers to account for the moneys received therefor.

An act in relation to holding Probate Courts during the present war.

An act to amend an act to provide for an additional issue of Treasury Notes.

An act to extend the provisions of an act entitled an act for the relief of Gen. William E. Anderson and others, approved December 10th, 1862.

An act for the relief of Edward Jordan, Sheriff of Taylor county.

An act relating to property confiscated to the use of the State.

An act to raise the salary of the State Treasurer and other officers therein named.

An act providing for the payment of certain claims against the State.

An act to amend the Charter of the Alabama & Florida Railroad Company.

An act more particularly defining the duties of Tax Assessors and Collectors in this State.

An act for the relief of Margaret J. McKeown, widow of James A. McKeown.

An act for the relief of D. B. Cappleman, Sheriff of Marion county.

An act to incorporate the Monticello and Thomasville Railroad.

An act to amend the Patrol laws of this State.

An act to authorize the Clerk of the Circuit Court of Sumter county to keep his office at his own house.

An act to amend the Charter of the Florida, Atlantic & Gulf Central Railroad Company.

An act for the relief of Albert Hyer.

An act relative to claims placed in the hands of District Solicitors of this State.

An act to assist the faithful and necessary enforcement of the Impressment Act of Congress, and to protect and defend the citizens of this State from oppression and unlawful acts of persons violating the said act, or claiming to act under the authority of the Confederate Government.

An act to aid the Confederate Government in the detection of frauds.

An act to be entitled an act to amend the election laws of this State relative to soldiers voting.

An act in relation to forfeited bonds of criminals.

An act to be entitled an act to legalize the acts of Samuel Lowe, acting Clerk of the Circuit Court.

An act to provide for the payment for Plats furnished the counties of Clay, Jackson and Calhoun.

An act to provide for the relief of Soldiers' Families and others that require assistance.

An act to appropriate ten thousand dollars for the Wayside Homes or Hospitals in this State.

An act to prevent and punish all persons planting and cultivating, in the State of Florida, over a certain quantity of land in Cotton and Tobacco during the continuance of the present war.

An act to prevent the distilling of Spirituous Liquors in this State.

An act for the relief of Aaron W. DaCosta.

An act further defining the duties of the Treasurer of the State.

An act to provide for furnishing to each Regiment and Battalion in Confederate service from this State a suitable Flag or Ensign, also a Flag to be used at the Capitol.

An act to provide Clothing for Troops from Florida in the service of the Confederate States.

An act making appropriations for the expenses of the Second Session of the Twelfth General Assembly, and for other purposes.

An act to amend an act to prevent the entry of lands occupied by Soldiers or their Families during the continuance of the present war, and also to regulate the entry and sale of Public Lands, approved Dec. 13th, 1862.

RESOLUTIONS.

Resolution of thanks to our Soldiers.

Resolution asking the Governor not to license any more Distilleries until the further action of the Legislature.

Resolutions of thanks to Gen. Wm. Bailey and Dr. Henry Bacon.

Resolutions relating to the appointment of Agent for Soldiers' Families in the counties of Santa Rosa and Escambia.

Resolution relative to Tax in Kind.

Resolution setting apart a Day of Fasting, Humiliation and Prayer.

Joint resolution relative to our sick or wounded Soldiers in Gen. Bragg's army.

Resolution for the destruction of the State Bonds on hand of the issues of 1856 and 1861.

Resolution relative to Confederate Treasury Notes.

Resolution relative to the civil authority of the State of Florida.

Joint resolution authorizing the Joint Committee on Finance and Public Accounts to destroy a sum of money therein named.

Joint resolution relative to the Arsenal.

Joint resolution in relation to the unsettled accounts of Ex-Gov. M. S. Perry, Quarter Master General H. V. Snell, and John W. Pearson, Disbursing Agent.

Resolution in relation to the accounts of the late United States Receivers and Registers.

Resolution in relation to copying the Laws.

Joint resolution relative to the pay of the Soldiers of the Confederate States.

Joint resolution in relation to exempting the Workmen and persons employed in the Jefferson Manufacturing Company.

Resolution in reference to exportation and importation of certain articles by private enterprise.

Resolutions relative to appointment of Agents in Greenville and Montgomery.

Resolution in relation to the war between the Confederate States and the United States.

LAWS OF THE STATE OF FLORIDA,

Second Session of the Twelfth General Assembly, 1863.

JOHN MILTON, Governor. B. F. ALLEN, Secretary of State. WALTER GWYNN, Comptroller of Public Accounts. C. H. AUSTIN, Treasurer. J. B. GALBRAITH, Attorney General. E. J. VANN, President of the Senate. J. B. WHITEHURST, Secretary of the Senate. T. J. EPPES, Speaker of the House. T. B. BAREFOOT, Clerk of the House.

CHAPTER 1,384—[No. 1.]

AN ACT to repeal an act entitled an act to regulate Trade and Intercourse with the Indians.

SECTION 1. *Be it enacted by the Senate and House of Representatives of the State of Florida in General Assembly convened,* That an act entitled an act to regulate trade and intercourse with the Indians, approved December 12th, 1862, be and the same is hereby repealed.

Passed the Senate November 20, 1863. Passed the House of Representatives November 21, 1863. Approved by the Governor November 24, 1863.

CHAPTER 1,385—[No. 2.]

AN ACT authorizing publication to be made out of the State of sales by Administrators and Executors in certain cases.

SECTION 1. *Be it enacted by the Senate and House of Representatives of the State of Florida in General Assembly convened,* That in all cases where the law requires Administrators or Executors to advertise in some newspaper any proceedings in relation

1863.

to estates in their charge, the same may be done in the newspapers most convenient to the county in which the estate, in question may be situated, whether said paper is published in or out of the State.

Passed the Senate November 20, 1863. Passed the House of Representatives November 24, 1863. Approved by the Governor November 25, 1863.

CHAPTER 1,386—[No. 3.]

AN ACT to change the place of holding the Circuit Court for Putnam county.

SECTION 1. *Be it enacted by the Senate and House of Representatives of the State of Florida in General Assembly convened,* That the Judge of the Circuit Court is authorized and is hereby required to hold the Courts for Putnam county at the Church near Sweet Water Branch, in the Moate's neighborhood, in said county, at the regular time appointed for holding such Court, until such time as it may be deemed safe by the presiding Judge to hold the same in Palatka.

Place of holding Court.

Passed the House of Representatives November 20, 1863. Passed the Senate November 23, 1863. Approved by the Governor November 25, 1863.

CHAPTER 1,387—[No. 4.]

AN ACT to amend Ordinance No. 53 of the Convention, in relation to Soldiers voting.

SECTION 1. *Be it enacted by the Senate and House of Representatives of the State of Florida in General Assembly convened,* That Ordinance No. 53 of the State Convention be and the same is hereby so amended as to allow soldiers from this State, in the military service of this State and the Confederate States, to vote for all county officers of the respective counties in which they reside, and also for Governor of the State, in the manner already provided for by law for soldiers voting for members of the General Assembly or for Representatives in the Congress of the Confederate States.

Soldiers may vote for Governor and county officers.

Passed the House of Representatives November 20, 1863. Passed the Senate November 23, 1863. Approved by the Governor November 25, 1863.

CHAPTER 1,388—[No. 5.]

AN ACT for the protection of Cattle Owners in the counties of Levy, Lafayette, Taylor, Wakulla and Duval.

SECTION 1. *Be it enacted by the Senate and House of Representatives of the State of Florida in General Assembly convened,* That from and after the passage of this act, it shall not be lawful for any person or persons to pen and part the cows and calves of another for the purpose of milking, or to milk them without the conset of the owners, in the counties of Levy, Taylor, Lafayette and Wakulla.

Penning cattle of others prohibited.

SEC. 2. *Be it further enacted,* That any person or persons so offending, shall be guilty of a misdemeanor, and upon conviction, shall be fined in a sum not exceeding one hundred dollars nor less than ten dollars.

Penalty

SEC. 3. *Be it further enacted,* That all laws or parts of laws conflicting with the provisions of this act be and the same are hereby repealed.

Repeal.

Passed the House of Representatives November 19, 1863. Passed the Senate November 24, 1863. Approved by the Governor November 27, 1863.

CHAPTER 1,389—[No. 6.]

AN ACT amending the Charter of the City of Pensacola.

WHEREAS, The evacuation of the City of Pensacola by the people, on account of circumstances growing out of the present war, has left said City without a government; and, whereas, when the people again return to their homes, a doubt may arise as to what course it is proper to pursue to again establish a government for the City—Therefore,

Preamble.

SECTION 1. *Be it enacted by the Senate and House of Representatives of the State of Florida in General Assembly convened,* That until the election herein provided, F. B. Bobe shall be Mayor of said City of Pensacola and shall be and is hereby authorized to perform all the duties appertaining to said office, as prescribed in the Charter of said City.

Mayor

SEC. 2. *Be it further enacted,* That until the election herein provided, Joseph Sierra, G. W. Hutton, W. H. Judah, C. L. Le-Baron, C. G. Barclay, James Knowles and Benj. D. Wright shall constitute the Board of Aldermen of the City of Pensacola, and said Aldermen shall be and they are hereby authorized to

Aldermen.

2

perform such duties appertaining to said office as may be required to protect the interests of the said City in this emergency.

Sec. 3. *Be it further enacted,* Should a vacancy occur in the office of Mayor, or in the office of Aldermen, by death, resignation or otherwise, the Board of Aldermen may fill such vacancy.

Vacancies.

Sec. 4. *Be it further enacted,* That it shall be the duty of the Mayor to call meetings of the Board whenever in his opinion the interest of the City of Pensacola may be promoted thereby, or when any five members of the Board may request a meeting of said Board to be called, and all acts done by the Mayor or under the direction of the Board shall be as valid as though performed within the corporate limits of the City of Pensacola.

Meetings of the Board.

Sec. 5. *Be it further enacted,* That within six months from the conclusion of a peace, it shall be the duty of the Board of Aldermen to order an election for Mayor and Board of Aldermen for the City of Pensacola, which election shall be governed by the rules and regulations heretofore in force, and the persons so elected shall hold their offices until their successors are elected and qualified, as required by the Charter to which this is an amendment.

Elect'n of May'r and Alderm'n

Sec. 6. *Be it further enacted,* That in the election herein provided no one shall be allowed to vote who had not resided within the corporate limits of the City of Pensacola for twelve months prior to the first day of May, 1862, with the intention of becoming a citizen of said City.

Voters.

Sec. 7. *Be it further enacted,* That upon the election and induction into office of the Mayor and Board of Aldermen herein provided, the municipal affairs of said City shall be governed by the same laws, ordinances and resolutions as were in force at the time of the evacuation of said City in May, 1862, the government of said City to be in all respects restored as nearly as practicable to the condition it was in at the time of the evacuation in May, 1862.

Laws and ordinances.

Sec. 8. *Be it further enacted,* That should the Board of Aldermen fail to call an election, as provided in this act, ten or more of the citizens of the City of Pensacola, qualified to vote at the election as provided in this Act, may proceed to order an election for Mayor and Board of Aldermen, such notice and the proceedings under it to be governed by the rules prescribed in the Charter, to which this is an amendment, regulating the election and prescribing the duties of Mayor and Board of Aldermen.

In case of failure to call election.

Passed the House of Representatives November 24, 1863. Passed the Senate November 24, 1863. Approved by the Governor November 27, 1863.

CHAPTER 1,390—[No. 7.]

AN ACT for the relief of James W. Johnson of Taylor county.

WHEREAS, It appears the widow of Isaiah Smith, of the county
of Taylor, has recently become insane, thereby creating much
trouble to her friends to take care of her, *Preamble.*

SECTION 1. *Be it therefore enacted by the Senate and House
of Representatives of the State of Florida in General Assembly convened,* That from and after the passage of this act, that
James W. Johnson, the brother of said widow Smith, be and he
is hereby authorized to receive ten dollars per month for the
taking care of and maintaining such widow and lunatic until *Care of lunatic.*
such time as her case can be brought before the Circuit Judge
and properly provided for as directed by law, such appropriation
to be made from the Treasury out of any monies not otherwise
appropriated, and charged to the lunatic fund, any law to the
contrary notwithstanding.

Passed the House of Representatives November 23, 1863. Passed the Senate
November 24, 1863. Approved by the Governor November 27, 1863.

CHAPTER 1,391—[No. 8.]

AN ACT to change the line dividing the counties of Suwannee and Columbia.

SECTION 1. *Be it enacted by the Senate and House of Representatives of the State of Florida in General Assembly convened,*
That the line dividing said counties where it strikes Section sixteen (16) in Township three (3) South of Range fifteen East shall
turn and run due East to the North-East corner of the North-
East quarter of said section, thence due South to the South-East *Boundary line.*
corner of said quarter Section, thence due West to where it will
strike the line now dividing said counties, so as to include the
entire town of Welburn, in the county of Suwannee, according to
the plan of said town, and that the inhabitants thereof be held
and considered citizens of Suwannee county.

Passed the House of Representatives November 23, 1863. Passed the Senate
November 24, 1863. Approved by the Governor November 27, 1863.

CHAPTER 1,392—[No. 9.]

AN ACT to amend the Charter of the City of Pensacola so as to authorize said City to aid in the construction of certain Railroads.

SECTION 1. *Be it enacted by the Senate and House of Representatives of the State of Florida in General Assembly convened,* That the City of Pensacola be and the same is hereby authorized to aid in the construction of a Railroad from the City of Pensacola, or some point on the line of the Alabama and Florida Railroad to the Apalachicola river, such aid to be given by subscription, endorsement of bonds or otherwise as the Board of Aldermen may determine, and not to exceed in amount five hundred thousand dollars.

SEC. 2. *Be it further enacted,* That before any obligation shall be entered into for furnishing this aid, the question as to whether the aid contemplated to be given shall be rendered shall be submitted to the qualified voters of said city, after ten days public notice, in such manner as the Board of Aldermen may prescribe, and if two-thirds of those voting shall be in favor of granting the aid asked for, it shall be the duty of the Mayor and Board of Aldermen to pursue the course necessary to carry into effect the wish of the people.

SEC. 3. *Be it further enacted,* That the City of Pensacola be and the same is hereby authorized to aid in the construction of a Railroad from the City of Pensacola, or some point on the line of the Alabama and Florida Railroad, to the City of Selma, Alabama, such aid to be given by subscription, endorsement of bonds or otherwise as the Board of Alderman may determine, and not to exceed in amount five hundred thousand dollars; the same course to be pursued with regard to the aid to be furnished as is prescribed in the second section of this act.

SEC. 4. *Be it further enacted,* That the vote of the citizens of Pensacola upon any one proposition which may be submitted to them shall not be conclusive as to any other proposition, but if the Board of Aldermen think proper, propositions for aid may be submitted in various forms for reception or rejection by the people.

Passed the Senate November 25, 1863. Passed the House of Representetives November 26, 1863. Approved by the Governer November 27, 1863.

marginal notes:
City authorized to aid in construction of railroad.

Question to be submitted to the citizens.

Railroad to Selma, Ala.

Amount of subscription.

Vote of citizens

CHAPTER 1,393—[No. 10.]

AN ACT to incorporate the Apalachicola Channel Company.

SECTION 1. *Be it enacted by the Senate and House of Repre-*

sentatives of the State of Florida in General Assembly convened, That John D. Atkins, Joseph L. Dunham, H. R. Taylor, W. T. Wood, George Buckman, C. G. Holmes, A. Hancock, Thomas Orman, R. Myers, T. H. Austin, F. M. Bryan and W. J. McAllister, citizens of the Confederate States and of this State, and such persons as now are and may be hereafter associated with them, not less than ten in number, of whom at least five shall be residents of this State, shall be and are hereby constituted and declared to be a body politic and corporate, by name and style of the Apalachicola Channel Company, for the purpose of deepening or constructing a channel affording a greater depth of water for vessels of all classes from the City of Apalachicola, extending from the up river limits of the corporation of Apalachicola out to deep water in St. George's Sound, as far as they may think advisable, or in said Sound wherever they may think necessary. And by that name they, their successors and assigns, shall be capable in law of suing and being sued, plead and being impleaded, answering and being answered unto, defending and being defended in all courts, tribunals and places whatsoever, and shall have power to adopt, make and use (a) common seal, and the same at pleasure to change, alter and amend; and they and their successors and their assigns, by the same manner and style, shall be capable of creating, purchasing, renting or leasing wharf lots adjacent to the channel and erecting thereon wharves where none exist; but in no case shall they have the power or the right to interfere with or obstruct any private or city wharf, or wharf lot, or otherwise injure any private property or vested right of individuals, or of the City of Apalachicola; of purchasing, renting or leasing any wharf or wharves now built or erected, but shall always conform to the rates of wharfage established by the City of Apalachicola, and shall be subject and liable to all the rules and regulations of said City established for the regulation of anchorage and quarantine, with the privilege and right in said company of purchasing, holding and conveying any property, real or personal, any steamer or steamers, (or steamers,) vessel or vessels, barges or boats of any kind or description whatsoever, necessary or expedient to carry out and fulfill the objects of said corporation.

SEC. 2. *Be it further enacted,* The capital of said company shall be two hundred thousand dollars, divided into shares of one hundred dollars each, transferable in such manner and under such restrictions as the said corporation by their by-laws may require and direct.

SEC. 3. *Be it further enacted,* That the above named persons, or a majority of them, as Commissioners, may open books to receive subscriptions to the capital stock of said corporation, at such time or times and place or places, as soon after peace is de-

Corporators.

Style and purpose of Co.

Corporate powers.

Capital stock.

Books of subscription.

Meeting of stock-holders.

Election of Directors.

Annu'l meeting of Stockhold-ers.

Pres dent.

Vacancies.

Secretary.

Failure to organize in time no cause of dissolution.

clared as they, or a majority of them, may think proper; and as soon as fifty per centum upon the capital stock shall be sub-scribed, and twenty per centum paid in, to give notice for a meeting of the Stockholders to choose five Directors among said Stockholders, three of whom, at least, shall be citizens of the State of Florida, and such election shall be made at the time and place appointed by such of the Stockholders as shall attend for the purpose, either in person or by proxy, each share of the capi-tal stock entitling the holder thereof to one vote. And the said above named persons, or a majority of them, shall be inspectors of the first election of Directors of said corporation, and shall certify under their hands the names of those persons duly elected. And the Commissioners shall deliver over the subscription book, with all funds in hand, to said Directors, who may keep the same open by a vote of the majority of Stockholders for further sub-scription, if the same be deemed expedient, until the entire amount of capital stock shall be subscribed; and each Stock-holder so subscribing, after organization of said corporation as aforesaid, shall be bound by said election and organization until the next annual election in course, as is hereinafter provided, when he shall be entitled to vote as original Stockholder.

SEC. 4. *Be it further enacted,* That there shall be an annual meeting of the Stockholders of said corporation, at such time and place as the said corporation may provide by its by-laws, for the purpose of electing Directors; and that the time of holding the first meeting of the Directors under the said first election shall be fixed by the said Directors, or a majority of them; and the said Directors chosen at said election, or at the annual elec-tion to be afterwards held, shall, as soon as may be, after every subsequent election, choose out of their number a President, and in case of the death, resignation or removal of the President, or any Director, such vacancy or vacancies may be filled for the remainder of the year wherein they may happen by the said remaining Directors, or a majority of them; and, in case of the absence of the President, the said Directors, or a majority of them, may appoint a President "*pro tem.,*" who shall exercise such powers and functions as the by-laws of said corporation may provide.

SEC. 5. *Be it further enacted,* That the said Directors, or a majority of them, shall elect, simultaneously with the President and annually, a suitable person, other than a Director, who shall discharge the duties of Secretary and Treasurer of said corpora-tion, who shall be a Stockholder in the same.

SEC. 6. *Be it further enacted,* That in case it should happen that an election of Directors should not be made when pursuant to this act it should be had, the said corporation shall not by reason thereof be dissolved, but such election shall be held at any other time, and the Directors previously elected shall continue as Directors until a new election shall be had, a majority of said Directors of said corporation to transact all business of said 'corporation; and they shall have power to call in the capital stock of said Company by such instalments as they may deem advisable, giving thirty days notice thereof to the Stockholders, by advertisement, in some newspaper or newspapers. In case of the non-payment of said instalments, the Stockholders so failing to pay their instalments, within ten days after the same becomes due, shall forfeit their share or shares and the amount before paid to the corporation. *Instalments of stock.*

SEC. 7. *Be it further enacted*, That said Company may levy and collect tonnage dues upon all vessels which shall pass through said channel constructed or deepened under this act, which shall draw over six feet water, not exceeding one dollar per ton for the first ten years after the construction or deepening of said channel, and not exceeding fifty cents per ton for the succeeding ten years; same tonnage duties shall entitle all vessels to proceed to and from the City of Apalachicola back to deep water at the rate aforesaid, and said tonnage rates may be collected by attachment, which may be commenced without giving bonds. *Tonnage dues, how collected.*

SEC. 8. *Be it further enacted*, That said Company shall have a lien upon all vessels, their tackle, apparel and furniture, passing through said channel for the collection and recovery of the channel duties aforesaid. *Lien upon vessels.*

SEC. 9. *Be it further enacted*, That the said Company shall, from time to time, appoint such Captains, Commanders, Agents, and all other officers and employees as to them may seem proper and necessary for the interest of said corporation. *Officers of Company.*

SEC. 10. *Be it further enacted*, That the Directors of said Company, or a majority of them, shall settle and adjust the books and accounts of said corporation at least once every year, and submit a detailed statement of the affairs thereof to the Stockholders at their annual meeting, and declare and pay such dividend of the actual profits thereof as the condition of the said Company may justify; and the Stockholders shall have power to adopt such by-laws for the government of said Company as they may deem proper, not inconsistent with the charter or the laws of the State of Florida. *Books and accounts.* *Dividends.* *By-laws.*

SEC. 11. *Be it further enacted*, That the said Directors, or a majority them, shall have power to exact from the Treasurer, or any other officer of said Company, a bond in such sum as they may deem proper, conditioned for the faithful performance of the duties of the office. *Bond of officers.*

SEC. 12. *Be it further enacted*, That the private property of the Stockholders in said Company shall only be liable for the *Private property of stockh'drs* debts, liabilities and obligations of said Company *pro rata*, according to the amount of stock owned by each Stockholder.

Passed the Senate November 25, 1863. Passed the House of Representatives November 26, 1863. Approved by the Governor November 27, 1863.

Chapter 1,394—[No. 11.]

AN ACT to be entitled an act to allow the Judges of the Circuit Courts of this State to appoint Sheriffs in certain cases.

SECTION 1. *Be it enacted by the Senate and House of Representatives of the State of Florida in General Assembly convened,* That whenever any Sheriff or Coroner in this State shall fail to attend in person, or by deputy, any term of the Circuit Court of his county, from sickness, death or other cause, the Circuit Judge attending said Court shall have power to appoint a Sheriff, who shall assume all the responsibilites, perform all the duties and receive the same compensation as if he had been duly elected the Sheriff for said term of the Court and no longer.

Court may appoint Sheriff.

SEC. 2. *Be it further enacted,* That all laws militating against this act be and the same are hereby repealed.

Passed the Senate November 19, 1863. Passed the House of Representatives November 21, 1863. Approved by the Governor November 27, 1863.

Chapter 1,395—[No. 12.]

AN ACT to amend the sixth Section of an act entitled an act to change the mode of selecting Grand and Petit Jurors in this State, approved February 8 1861.

SECTION 1. *Be it enacted by the Senate and House of Representatives of the State of Florida in General Assembly convened,* That it shall not be necessary to revise the Jury lists of the several counties of this State at every term of the Circuit Courts as now provided by law, but the same shall be revised at the Fall term of the Circuit Courts of the several counties in this State in each and every year.

Revisal of jury lists.

SEC. 2. *Be it further enacted,* That the Judges of the Circuit Courts of this State be and they are hereby authorized to take from the Jury Box (Grand and Petit,) the names of all persons

Persons in military service.

in the military service of the Confederate States, or who may hereafter enter the military service of the Confederate States, and seal the same up in an envelope, to be safely kept by the Court so long as said person remains in said service; and at the expiration of such service their names to be returned to the Jury Box from which they were taken.

Passed the House of Representatives November 23, 1863. Passed the Senate November 26, 1863. Approved by the Governor November 30, 1863.

CHAPTER 1,396—[No. 13.]

AN ACT to legalize entries of Public Lands made after the Secession of Florida and requiring the Receivers to account for the moneys received therefor.

SECTION 1. *Be it enacted by the Senate and House of Representatives of the State of Florida in General Assembly convened,* That all entries and land warrants locations made upon the public lands of this State at any of the late United States land offices after the tenth day of January, 1861, be and they are hereby confirmed and legalized, and such lands shall be patented to the purchasers and locators upon the surrender by them of the duplicate receipt or certificates of location issued to them.

Entries after January 10, 1861 confirmed.

SEC. 2. *Be it further enacted,* That the Register of Public Lands shall ask and demand of the late United States Receivers the payment to him of all monies received by them from sales of public lands after the tenth day of January, 1861, except so much as has been refunded to the purchasers; and in case of a failure or refusal to pay the same, the Register of Public Lands is hereby authorized and instructed to institute suit in the name of the State of Florida for the recovery thereof, before the Circuit Court of the county wherein such defaulting Receiver may reside, and the Solicitor of the Circuit shall prosecute such suit.

Monies receiv'd in payment for lands.

SEC. 3. *Be it further enacted,* That when the Receivers shall have paid to the Register of Public Lands the monies received by them as aforesaid, the Treasurer of the State shall pay to such Receivers the amount of salary and commissions that they would have been entitled to under the laws of the United States from the 10th day of January to the 27th day of April, 1861, said amount to be paid upon the warrant of the Register of Public Lands.

Salaries of Receivers.

Passed the House of Representatives November 20, 1863. Passed the Senate November 26, 1866. Approved by the Governor November 30, 1863.

3

CHAPTER 1,397—[No. 14.]

AN ACT in relation to holding Probate Courts during the present war.

SECTION 1. *Be it enacted by the Senate and House of Representatives of the State of Florida in General Assembly convened,* That from after the passage of this act, and until the close of the war, it shall be lawful for the Judge of Probate for the county of Santa Rosa, by giving due public notice as required by law, to hold his Court at Pine Level in said county.

In the county of Santa Rosa.

SEC. 2. *Be it further enacted,* That the said Judge of Probate shall keep a book of record of his proceedings, which shall, after the termination of the present war, be transcribed upon the original book of records of said county, and that he is hereby authorized to do the same.

Book of records

SEC. 3. *Be it further enacted,* That whenver the county site of any county in this State is in danger on account of the presence of the enemy, or on account of there being no military force sufficient to protect the same, it shall be lawful for the Judge of Probate of the county where such county site is in danger, to hold his Court and remove the records to any place in the county, or in an adjacent county, which may be the most convenient and safe, upon giving public notice, by posting in three public places in the county, or in some newspaper in this State.

Judges of Probate may remove records, &c., in case of public danger.

Passed the Senate November 26, 1863. Passed the House of Representatives November 27, 1863. Approved by the Governor November 30, 1863.

CHAPTER 1,398—[No. 15.]

AN ACT to amend an Act to provide for an additional issue of Treasury Notes.

SECTION 1. *Be it enacted by the Senate and House of Representatives of the State of Florida in General Assembly convened,* That the Governor be and he is hereby authorized to issue Treasury Notes or Change Bills of one dollar and of the fractional parts of a dollar, to the amount of fifty thousand dollars, in lieu of the " fifty thousand dollars in hundreds" provided for in the first section of the act entitled an act to provide for an additional issue of Treasury Notes, approved December 13, 1862.

Change bills.

SEC. 2. *Be it further enacted,* That all laws and parts of laws conflicting with this act, be and they are hereby repealed.

Passed the Senate November 23, 1863. Passed the House of Representatives November 27, 1863. Approved by the Governor November 30, 1863.

CHAPTER 1,399—[No. 16.]

AN ACT to extend the provisions of an Act entitled an Act for the relief of General William E. Anderson and others, approved December 10th, 1862.

SECTION 1. *Be it enacted by the Senate and House of Representatives of the State of Florida in General Assembly convened*, That the Comptroller of the State be and he is hereby required to audit and allow, and the Treasurer is hereby required to pay upon warrant from the Comptroller, all amounts found due to persons acting under the orders of General William E. Anderson for services rendered in the transportation of arms, ammunition, &c., from Marianna to Neil's landing, in Jackson county, or for provisions furnished to Capt. J. M. F. Erwin's company, or others, whilst guarding, discharging and transporting said arms and ammunition from the Steamer Florida, at St. Andrews Bay, to Marianna, in the county aforesaid, under and by virtue of an order from his Excellency the Governor of this State to the said General Anderson: *Provided*, That the whole amount of expenditure, under the provision of this act, shall not exceed the sum of two hundred dollars.

Comptroller to issue warrant.

Passed the House of Representatives November 24, 1863. Passed the Senate November 24, 1863. Approved by the Governor November 30, 1863.

CHAPTER 1,400—[No. 17.]

AN ACT for the relief of Edward Jordan, Sheriff of Taylor County.

WHEREAS, Edward Jordan, Sheriff of said county, was charged with one hundred dollars revenue for license to retail spirituous liquors in Taylor County, Florida, and was compelled to pay the same or be in default; Whereas, he was not indebted but fifty dollars of the amount,

Preamble.

SECTION 1. *Therefore be it enacted by the Senate and House of Representatives of the State of Florida in General Assembly convened*, That the Comptroller of the State be and he is hereby authorized to issue his warrant upon the Treasurer of the State for the sum of fifty dollars, in favor of Edward Jordan, to be paid out of any money in the Treasury not otherwise appropriated, any law to the contrary notwithstanding.

Comptroller to issue warrant.

Passed the House of Representatives November 24, 1863. Passed the Senate November 26, 1863. Approved by the Governor November 30, 1863.

CHAPTER 1,401—[No. 18.]

AN ACT relating to property confiscated to the use of the State.

SECTION 1. *Be it enacted by the Senate and House of Representatives of the State of Florida in General Assembly convened,* That all loyal citizens of the Confederate States of America having claims or demands, obligations or debts of any and every kind, against any person or under acceptance for any person late a citizen of the State of Florida, and whose property has been or may hereafter be seized and confiscated by the judgment of the Circuit Courts under ordinance number thirty-nine (39) of the late Convention of the State, or under any other ordinance of said Convention, shall be permitted to intervene by petition before the Court ordering the confiscation, and to have decreed him or them the amount of his or their claim, demand, obligation, acceptance or debt, upon proof of the same being made and submitted to the Court, and to have execution therefor as in cases of judgment.

Persons having claims against confiscated property.

Manner of proceeding.

SEC. 2. *Be it further enacted,* That the several Judges of the Circuit Courts of the State are hereby directed to entertain all applications under this act, and to give judgment therein at Chambers, when the cause or causes are ready for hearing.

Judge may entertain causes at chambers.

SEC. 3. *Be it further enacted,* That in case the property, or any portion thereof, consists of money, and the same has been deposited in the Treasury of the State, the order of the Judge directed to the Treasurer shall be sufficient voucher for its payment; and the Comptroller is hereby ordered to audit and the Treasurer to pay the amount so directed to be paid by the order of the Judge aforesaid.

Manner of paying claims.

SEC. 4. *Be it further enacted,* That upon all petitions presented under this act the decree shall direct a pro rata payment upon each judgment, unless there are funds or property sufficient to satisfy all: *Provided, however,* That where a lien is alleged and proved against any particular fund, then said lien shall have preference and be paid in full, irrespective of all other claims : *And, provided further,* That all petitions claiming the benefit of such pro rata division shall be filed within sixty days after public notice in the newspapers of the judgment of confiscation.

Payment pro rata.

SEC. 5. *Be it further enacted,* That after the payment of any and all such claims as provided in the foregoing sections, or in cases where no claims are presented as authorized in this bill, the next of kin in the direct ascending and descending lines of any person falling or coming under the provisions of the ordinance number thirty-nine (39,) referred to in the first section of this act, faithful citizens of the Confederate States, or engaged in their military or naval service, shall be entitled to have decreed them (they paying all costs) the property, effects and credits of such person so departing the State, as set out and provided in the aforesaid ordinance number thirty-nine (39,) as if dead intestate, leaving no other heirs, or distributees, chargeable, however, in their hands, as in case of administration or heirship, with all debts due to faithful citizens of any of the Confederate States, as provided for in this bill. *Distribution of residue to next of kin.*

SEC. 6. *Be it further enacted*, That the Judges of the Circuit Courts shall have power and authority, in all cases arising under the said ordinance number 39, to fix and order and decree that all expenses, fees, costs, &c., which the State may incur, that may accrue and arise in any such cases on petition or otherwise, shall be paid out of the funds arising from the sale of such confiscated property, or such cash funds as may be in hand arising in such case ; and such order shall authorize and be an appropriation of such funds as may be necessary and proper for said purpose. *Costs. fees, &c.*

SEC. 7. *Be it further enacted*, That the Attorney General be and he is hereby required to give the notice by publication provided for by the 4th section of this act. *Notice.*

SEC. 8. *Be it further enacted*, That whenever the State of Florida has a claim or demand against such person, other than the claim derived from the judgment of confiscation, or any citizen thereof has any claim, whether liquidated or unliquidated, the Court shall hear and determine the same at Chambers on petition, and give a decree thereon, to be paid out of said confiscated property, before the heirs shall take as aforesaid. *Claims against fund by State.*

Passed the House of Representatives November 24, 1863. Passed the Senate November 25, 1863. Approved by the Governor November 30, 1863.

CHAPTER 1,402—[No. 19.]

AN ACT to raise the salary of the State Treasurer and other Officers therein named.

· SECTION 1. *Be it enacted by the Senate and House of Representatives of the State of Florida in General Assembly convened*, That from and after the passage of this act, the salary of the State Treasurer shall be sixteen hundred dollars per annum, payable as heretofore provided by law. *Treasurer.*

SEC. 2. *Be it further enacted*, That the Attorney General and Clerk in the office of the Register of Public Lands shall each receive three hundred dollars in addition to the compensation now allowed by law ; and the Private Secretary of the Governor shall receive four hundred dollars in addition to the compensation *Attorney Gen'l & Clerk in Land Office, Private Sec'ty of Gov'r, Comptroller.*

now allowed by law; and that the Solicitors of the several Circuits receive two hundred dollars in addition to their present salaries; and that the Comptroller be allowed, in addition to his present salary, two hundred dollars.

SEC. 3. *Be it further enacted,* That the fees of Sheriffs, Clerks of the Circuit Courts and Judges of Probate shall be double the present fees allowed: *Provided,* That Jailors shall receive one dollar per day for each prisoner's subsistance.

Fees of Sheriff's, Clerks and Judges of Probate.

Passed the House of Representatives November 25, 1863. Passed the Senate November 27, 1863. Approved by the Governor November 30, 1863.

CHAPTER 1,403—[No. 20.]

AN ACT providing for the payment of certain Claims against the State.

SECTION 1. *Be it enacted by the Senate and House of Representatives of the State of Florida in General Assembly convened,* That the Comptroller be and he is hereby authorized and required to audit and allow the claims for services rendered and supplies furnished, arising out of the military operations of the State in 1861 and 1862, which claims are now in the hands of the Quarter Master General of the State, and have been approved and signed by one of the following named officers, viz: Brigadier General R. F. Floyd, Lt. Col. Thos. E. James, Major S. P. Richardson, Capt. John D. Atkins, Lt. R. D. Mann and Quarter Master J. J. Griffin, Walter J. Robinson, W. K. Hyer, H. K. Simmons and Joseph M. Taylor, Aid-de-Camp; and the Treasurer shall pay the same to the claimant, or his legally authorized agent, on the warrant of the Comptroller: *Provided,* The whole amount of expenditure under this bill shall not exceed the sum of five thousand and eighty-six ($5,086) dollars.

Claims to be paid.

Limitation.

SEC. 2. *Be it further enacted,* That no claim shall be paid under the provisions of this act except such as shall be endorsed by the Chairman of the Committee on Claims in the House, and Chairman of the Committee on Propositions and Grievances in the Senate.

Endorsement of claims.

Passed the House of Representatives November 25, 1863. Passed the Senate November 30, 1863. Approved by the Governor December 1, 1863.

CHAPTER 1,404—[No. 21.]

AN ACT to amend the Charter of the Alabama & Florida Railroad Company.

SECTION 1. *Be it enacted by the Senate and House of Representatives of the State of Florida in General Assembly convened,* That the Charter of the Alabama & Florida Railroad Company be and the same is hereby amended as follows: First, the name of said Company shall be changed to Pensacola Railroad Company, after notice shall have been given for three months in some newspaper printed in the City of Pensacola, which notice shall state the day on which said change of name shall commence to take effect: Second, said Railroad Company shall have power, with the assent of the Stockholders in general meeting, to aid in the construction of a building in the City of Pensacola to be used as a Hotel; also, shall have power to aid in the establishment of an Omnibus line in the City of Pensacola, and in the establishment of a line or lines of Steam Vessels, to run from the City or port of Pensacola to any other port or ports, this aid to be given by subscription or otherwise, and to such an amount as the Board of Directors may think proper.

Name of company changed.

Railroad hotel.

Line of steam vessels.

SEC. 2. *Be it further enacted,* That if from any cause the right of way has not been obtained by the Company, or when stone, lumber or other material are required in the construction or repairs of said Railroad, and the owner and the Company cannot agree upon the price, or when the owner is an infant, non resident or *non compos mentis,* then it shall be lawful for the President and Directors of said Company to apply to the Sheriff of the County in which said land or other property may be situated, who shall summon a jury of seven disinterested free holders, a majority of whom shall be authorized to assess the damages and return their award or judgment to the next term of the Circuit Court for the county in which said land or other property may be situated, and which shall be entered by the Clerk as the judgement of the Court, and execution may issue thereupon for the amount of said judgment and costs: *Provided, always,* That if either party shall, upon the return thereof, be dissatisfied, they may, upon filing bond, with good and sufficient security, in such sum as the Court may order, be allowed an appeal to the next term of the Circuit Court, when said case shall stand for trial *de novo: Provided, also,* Thirty days notice shall have been given to the opposite party, issued by the Clerk of the Court and served by the Sheriff of the county.

Proceeding in the nature of a writ of ad quod damnum.

SEC. 3. *Be it further enacted,* That the jurors summoned as aforesaid shall (before proceeding to the discharge of the duties herein required) take an oath or affirmation, which the Sheriff is

Oath of jurors.

hereby authorized to administer, to the effect that they will well and truly inquire into and to the best of their judgment assess the damages accruing to the owner or owners of such lands or materials, or lands and materials, by means of the proposed construction.

Property to inure to R. R. Co.

SEC. 4. *Be it further enacted,* That the said lands or other property so condemned or estimated as aforesaid shall inure to and become the property of said Company upon the payment by the said Company of the amount assessed by the jury to the party claiming damages on account of the construction of said Road through said lands, or for such other property: *Provided,* That said work shall be in no wise delayed on account of the proceedings had as aforesaid.

Passed the House of Representatives November 24, 1863. Passed the Senate November 24, 1863. Approved by the Governor, December 1, 1863.

CHAPTER 1,405—[No. 22.]

AN ACT more particularly defining the duties of Tax-Assessors and Collectors in this State.

SECTION 1. *Be it enacted by the Senate and House of Representatives of the State of Florida in General Assembly convened,* That from and after the passage of this act, it shall be the duty of all Tax-Assessors and Collectors in this State to proceed immediately after the first of January, in each and every year, to assess the tax on all taxable property in their respective counties, excepting such counties as may be controlled or partially controlled by the enemy; and shall each, as soon as the same is completed, proceed to make out three books in alphabetical order of all the taxable property in his county—one of which books he shall forward by the first day of July, in each and every year, to the Comptroller of Public Accounts of this State—one other of said books he shall deliver to the Board of County Commissioners of his county, the —— to be retained by himself.

Time of assessment.

Tax books.

Penalty of failure to return books.

SEC. 2. *Be it further enacted,* That any Tax-Assessor who shall fail to furnish the Board of County Commissioners or the Comptroller with a correct copy of the books so made out by him, on or before the time prescribed in the first section of this act, shall forfeit to the State all commissions for assessing and collecting taxes for said year, and shall forfeit the additional sum of one hundred dollars, to be recovered against him and securities in the manner now prescribed by law, under an act entitled "an act to facilitate the collection of debts due the State by any officers," approved December 15th, 1862; and the further sum of one hundred dollars for every additional month he shall fail to furnish said book or books to be collected as above prescribed.

SEC. 3. *Be it further enacted,* That an act entitled "an act relative to the assessment of taxes," approved December 8th, 1862, be and the same is hereby repealed.

Passed the Senate November 26, 1863. Passed the House of Representatives November 30, 1863. Approved by the Governor December 2, 1863.

CHAPTER 1,406—[No. 23.]

AN ACT for the relief of Margaret J. McKeown, widow of James A. McKeown.

SECTION 1. *Be it enacted by the Senate and House of Representatives of the State of Florida in General Assembly convened,* That the entry by James A. McKeown of the South East quarter of Section sixteen, in Township twenty-one South, of Range nineteen, East, shall be and the same is hereby set aside and cancelled; and upon the application of Margaret J. McKeown, the widow of said James A. McKeown, the Treasurer of the State is authorized and required to refund and pay over to her, from the *Treasurer of the* moneys in his hands belonging to the Common School Fund, *State pay.* the amounts paid for said tract of land, with interest from the dates of such payments upon warrants of the Comptroller of Public Accounts, which warrant shall be issued by said Comptroller upon the filing of a certificate of the Register of Public Lands, stating the amounts and dates of the payments aforesaid; and the Register of Public Lands is hereby authorized and required, upon demand of the said Margaret J. McKeown, to cancel and surrender the bonds now in his possession, which were executed by the said James A. McKeown, for credit instalments upon the entry of the land aforesaid.

Passed the Senate November 26, 1863. Passed the House of Representatives November 30, 1863. Approved by the Governor December 2, 1863.

CHAPTER 1,407—[No. 24.]

AN ACT for the relief of D. B. Cappleman, Sheriff of Marion county.

SECTION 1. *Be it enacted by the Senate and House of Representatives of the State of Florida in General Assembly convened,*

4

That the Comptroller be and he is hereby authorized and directed to remit a certain fine now outstanding against D. B. Cappleman,

Fine remitted. Sheriff of Marion county, in the case of the State of Florida vs. John F. McMonroe, the sum of said fine being $1,089 10-100 (one thousand and eighty-nine one-hundredths dollars.)

Passed the Senate November 27, 1863. Passed the House of Representatives November 30, 1863. Approved by the Governor December 2, 1863.

CHAPTER 1,408—[No. 25.]

AN ACT to incorporate the Monticello and Thomasville Railroad.

SECTION 1. *Be it enacted by the Senate and House of Representatives of the State of Florida in General Assembly convened,*.

Commission'rs. That J. Y. Jones, J. S. Divine, Robert Scott, Richard Turnbull, Richard Parkhill, F. R. Fildes, B. W. Bellamy and A. M. Manning, of the County of Jefferson, be and they are hereby appointed Commissioners to open books and receive subscriptions for stock in a Railroad to be constructed from the town of Monti-

Route. cello, by the most practicable route, to the Georgia line, in the direction of Thomasville, Georgia, any five of whom are author-

Books of subscription. ized to open books for the purpose of receiving subscriptions to the Capital Stock of said Company at such times (not exceeding nine months after the passage of this act) and places as they, or a majority of them, may think proper, upon giving public notice thereof of not less than twenty days, and shall keep the same open until the whole of the Capital Stock is subscribed.

SEC. 2. *Be it further enacted,* That the Capital Stock of said

Capital stock. Company may be three hundred thousand dollars, with the privilege of increasing the same to five hundred thousand dollars, should such an increase, in the judgment of the Directors of said Company, be found necessary for its construction and future man-

Shares. agement, and shall be divided into shares of one hundred dollars each.

SEC. 3. *Be it further enacted,* That said Railroad be and is hereby authorized to connect or intersect at the Georgia line with a Railroad to be constructed from Thomasville, Georgia.

SEC. 4. *Be it further enacted,* That as soon as seventy-five thousand dollars shall have been subscribed to the Capital Stock of said Company, the subscribers of said stock, their successors

Georgia connections. or assigns, shall be and are hereby declared to be incorporated into a Company, by the name of the Monticello and Thomasville Railroad Company, and by that name shall be capable of purchasing, holding, leasing and conveying real, personal and mixed property, so far as shall be necessary for the purpose of this Corporation, and by said incorporated name may sue and be sued, plead and be impleaded, answer and be answered unto in any Court of law or equity in this State, or elsewhere; and to have and use a common seal, and the same to alter or amend at pleasure; to pass all by-laws, rules and ordinances for the good government of said Corporation as to them may seem proper, and generally to do all things necessary to carry into effect the object of this act.

SEC. 5. *Be it further enacted,* That as soon as one hundred thousand dollars shall have been subscribed, and one-fifth part thereof paid in cash, the Commissioners hereby appointed, or a majority of them, shall call a meeting of the subscribers, at such time and place as they may appoint, and at such meeting the said subscribers, or those holding a majority of shares in said Company, shall elect by ballot seven Directors to manage the affairs of said Company, and the Commissioners aforesaid, or a majority of them, shall be judges of said first election of Directors, and the Directors thus chosen shall elect from among themselves a President of said Company, (who shall be allowed) such compensation as they may think proper, and on all occasions whenever a vote of Stockholders shall be taken, each Stockholder shall be allowed one vote for every share owned by him or her, and any Stockholder may depute in writing any other person to vote and act for him or her, as his or her proxy.

SEC. 6. *Be it further enacted,* That the said President and Directors shall be chosen annually by the Stockholders of said Company, and if any vacancy shall occur by death, resignation, or otherwise, of any President or Director before the year for which they were elected shall have expired, such vacancy shall be filled by the President and Directors, or a majority of them; and that the President and Directors shall hold their office until their successors are chosen and qualified, shall have power to call meetings of Stockholders at any time; and the Stockholders, by a majority of votes, may have power to remove the President or any Director, and to fill all vacancies occasioned by removal at pleasure.

SEC. 7. *Be it further enacted,* That the said President and Directors, or a majority of them, may appoint all such officers, engineers, agents or servants, whatsoever, as they may deem necessary to carry on the business of said Company, dismiss them at pleasure, and the majority of them shall determine the compensation of all said officers, engineers, agents and servants, shall have power to pass all by-laws which they may deem necessary and proper for exercising all the powers vested in this Company for carrying into effect the objects of this act: *Provided,* That such by-laws shall not be contrary to the laws of this State,

1863.

Loans.

or of the Confederate States, and said President and Directors, or a majority of them, are empowered to borrow money to carry into effect the objects of this act, to issue certificates or other evidences of said loan and to pledge the property of said Company for the payment of the same with the interest.

Instalments.

SEC. 8. *Be it further enacted*, That the said President and Directors shall have power to require the Stockholders of said Company to pay such instalments on their respective shares of stock, and at such times and places, either in money, materials, labor or provisions, as they may think best for the interests of said Company; and upon the refusal at any time of any Stockholder to pay the instalment required on his, her or their stock, in pursuance of any call made by the said President and Directors as aforesaid, said President and Directors may, upon giving thirty days notice, proceed to sell at public sale the share or shares of said stock owned by said Stockholder, or such part as they may think proper, to the highest bidder; and if upon a sale

Defaulting stockholders.

of shares of stock owned by said defaulting Stockholder, said stock should be sold for more than the amount due upon instalment as above mentioned, the excess, after deducting accruing interest and the necessary expenses of sale, shall be paid over to said defaulting Stockholder.

Lands, &c., for construction of road.

SEC. 9. *Be it further enacted*, That the President and Directors of said Company are hereby authorized to contract for and receive conveyances of land, stone, lumber, wood and all materials which may be necessary or required for the construction of said Railroad; and when the owner and Company cannot agree upon the price, or when the owner is an infant, non-resident or *non compus mentis*, or in any wise incapable or unable to manage or attend to his, her or their own affairs, then it shall be lawful for the President and Directors of said Company to apply to the Sheriff of the county in which said land or other property may be situated, who shall summon a jury of seven disinterested freeholders, a majority of whom shall be authorized to assess the

Ad quod damnum.

damages and return their award or judgment to the next term of the Circuit Court of the county in which said land or other property may be situated, which shall be entered by the Clerk as the judgment of the Court, and when by said Company payment of said judgment is made, the land so appropriated to the use of the Road may be used, owned and occupied by said Company for the use aforesaid : *Provided, always*, That if either party shall, upon the return thereof, be dissatisfied, they may, upon filing bond, with good and sufficient security, in such sum as the Court may order, be allowed an appeal to the next term of the Circuit Court of said county, when said case shall stand for trial *de novo : Provided, also*, Thirty days notice shall have been given to the opposite party, issued by the Clerk of the Court and served by the Sheriff of the county, and in no case shall such appeal so operate as to delay the progress of the work of said Railroad.

SEC. 10. *Be it further enacted,* That the persons summoned as aforesaid shall (before proceeding to discharge the duties herein required) take an oath or affirmation, which the Sheriff is hereby authorized to administer, to the effect that they will well and truly inquire into and to the best of their judgment assess the damages accruing to the owner or owners of such land, or materials, by means of the proposed construction, and that said lands or property so condemned and estimated, as aforesaid, shall become the property of said Company upon the payment of the damages assessed by said jury.

Oath of jury.

SEC. 11. *Be it further enacted,* That in case any person shall wilfully injure or obstruct in any degree the said Road or Roads, he shall forfeit and pay unto the said Company three times the amount of all damages it may sustain in consequence thereof, to be sued for and recovered before any Court having jurisdiction thereof; and, on complaint to any magistrate within whose jurisdiction such offence shall be committed, it shall be the duty of such magistrate to bind the person or persons so offending with sufficient security for his or their good behavior for the period of not less than one year; and such offender shall also be subject to indictment, and, on conviction, shall be sentenced, at the discretion of the Court, to not less than three or more than six months imprisonment.

Persons obstructing road.

SEC. 12. *Be it further enacted,* That after the completion of said Road, or any part thereof, the said President and Directors may lay and collect tolls from all persons, property, merchandize and other commodities transported thereon; *Provided,* The net profit of said Road shall not exceed twenty-five per centum per annum, and shall provide convenient passages to travel over said Road whenever it shall cross a public highway.

Tolls & profits.

SEC. 13. *Be it further enacted,* That said Company shall commence the building of said Road within three years, and complete the same within fifteen years, from the passage of this act.

Time of building road.

SEC. 14. *Be it further enacted,* That nothing in this act shall be construed as to confer upon said Company any right to . exercise the powers of a Banking Company, or to issue any description of paper intended for current circulation.

Banking prohibited.

SEC. 15. *Be it further enacted,* That certificates of stock shall be issued to the Stockholders on payment of each instalment, which shall be transferable on the Books of the Company only and by personal entry of the Stockholders, or his or her legal attorney or representative, duly authorized for that purpose.

Certifiactes of stock.

Passed the Senate November 27, 1863. Passed the House of Representatives December 1, 1863. Approved by the Governor December 3, 1863.

CHAPTER 1,409—[No. 26.]

AN ACT to amend the Patrol Laws of this State.

Persons subject to patrol duty.

SECTION 1. *Be it enacted by the Senate and House of Representatives of the State of Florida in General Assembly convened,* That the first section of an act to amend and consolidate the several acts of this State in relation to patrols, approved Dec. 17th, 1861, be and the same is hereby so amended as to include all persons between the ages of sixteen and sixty years, and such persons are hereby made subject to all patrol duty imposed by said act:

Proviso.

Provided, That the County Commissioners of their respective counties shall have the power to exempt from duty all persons who are physically disqualified for the duties imposed on them by the provisions of this act. That the provisions of this bill shall be in full force and effect during the continuance of the present war and no longer.

Passed the Senate December 2, 1863. Passed the House of Representatives December 3, 1863. Approved by the Governor December 3, 1863.

CHAPTER 1,410—[No. 27.]

AN ACT to authorize the Clerk of the Circuit Court of Sumter County to keep his office at his own house.

SECTION 1. *Be it enacted by the Senate and House of Representatives of the State of Florida in General Assembly convened,* That from and after the passage of this act that it shall be lawful for the Clerk of the Circuit Court of Sumter County, in this State, to keep his office at his own house in said county for the term of two years from the passage of this act.

Passed the Senate December 2, 1863. Passed the House of Representatives December 3, 1863. Approved by the Governor December 3, 1863.

CHAPTER 1,411—[No. 28.]

AN ACT to amend the Charter of the Florida, Atlantic and Gulf Central Railroad Company.

SECTION 1. *Be it enacted by the Senate and House of Representatives of the State of Florida in General Assembly convened,* That the fourth section of an act to amend an act entitled an act to incorporate the Florida, Atlantic and Gulf Central Railroad Company, approved January 7th, 1853, be amended as follows: That is to say, that every Stockholder in said Company shall be entitled to one vote for each share of stock which he or she may have subscribed for or own, less than one hundred shares, for every ten shares above one hundred one vote, and for every fifty shares over five hundred one vote: *Provided,* That this amendmendment shall not be of force until it shall have received the sanction of all the Stockholders.

Passed the Senate December 1, 1863. Passed the House of Representatives December 3, 1863. Approved by the Governor December 3, 1863.

CHAPTER 1,412—[No. 29.]

AN ACT for the relief of Albert Hyer.

WHEREAS, There is an unsettled claim of Albert Hyer for services performed by him as Quarter Master under the appointment of Gen. Chase, which account has been mislaid,

SECTION 1. *Be it enacted by the Senate and House of Representatives of the State of Florida in General Assembly convened,* That upon the presentation of duplicate accounts, and the approvl of the same by the Governor, the Comptroller shall issue his warrant for the amount and the Treasurer shall pay the same.

Passed the Senate November 30, 1863. Passed the House of Representatives December 1, 1863. Approved by the Governor December 3, 1863.

CHAPTER 1,413—[No. 30.]

AN ACT relative to claims placed in the hands of District Solicitors in this State.

SECTION 1. *Be it enacted by the Senate and House of Representatives of the State of Florida in General Assembly convened,* That from and after the passage of this act, it shall be the duty of the Comptroller of this State to charge the several District Solicitors of this State with all claims whatever which he may place in their hands for collection of money for and on behalf of the State, or which he may otherwise require them to collect.

SEC. 2. *Be it further enacted,* That said charges shall be evidence of indebtedness on the part of any Solicitor against whom any charge is made for the full amount of such claim to the State, until the same shall be collected and paid into the Treasury, or sued to insolvency; which fact of insolvency shall be certified by the Circuit Judge of his Circuit, or unless said Solicitor shall make it fully appear to the Comptroller that the failure to collect the same did not originate from any neglect of his.

SEC. 3. *Be it further enacted,* That it shall be the duty of the said Solicitors to make a report to the Comptroller, on the first Monday in January and July in each and every year, of the condition of all claims placed in his hands, or which he may have been required to prosecute and collect, whether the same is in suit or in judgment, or collected, and the probable solvency or insolvency of claims not collected, and shall at the same time pay over all monies which he may have collected belonging to the State; and the Comptroller shall not audit or allow any claim which any Solicitor may have against the State for service who shall fail to make the report herein required until the same shall be made as above required.

Report of Solicitors.

Comptroller may retain salary of Solicitor.

SEC. 4. *Be it further enacted,* That in addition to the salaries now allowed by law to Solicitors, they shall be entitled to charge and receive ten per cent. upon all monies actually collected and paid into the Treasury of this State: *Provided,* That the said Solicitors shall not be authorized to charge, upon claims accruing and placed in his hands from and after the passage of this act, more than five per cent. upon all monies actually collected and paid into the Treasury of the State: *And, provided further,* That nothing in this act shall be so construed as to authorize the Comptroller to refuse to audit and allow the claims of Solicitors against this State for services in consequence of making the charges against him as provided in the second section of this act, unless he shall fail to account for and pay over the same, as provided for the third section of this act: *And, provided further,* That, upon the election and qualification of the successor of any Solicitor in this State, the Solicitor going out of office shall deliver to the Solicitor elect a statement of all cases for the collection of money in favor of the State under his control, and the papers connected with the same, and take hs receipt for the same, which receipt, when filed with the Comptroller, shall release such Solicitor from any further liability to the State upon the claims receipted for; and the Solicitor receiving the claims shall be liable in all respects for the same, as provided against Solicitors in the second and third sections of this act.

Charges for collections, &c.

Statement of cases. Solicit'rs going out of office.

Passed the Senate November 25, 1863. Passed the House of Representatives December 2, 1863. Approved by the Governer December 3, 1863.

CHAPTER 1,414—[No. 31.]

AN ACT to assist the faithful and necessary enforcement of the Impressment Act of Congress, and to protect and defend the citizens of this State from oppression and unlawful acts of persons violating the said act or claiming to act under the authority of the Confederate Government.

WHEREAS, The manner in which Impressments are being made by persons claiming to act under the authority of the impressment act of the Confederate States has become a serious evil, unauthorized by the law, or by the Confederate authority, oppressive in its results, and destructive of the rights of the citizen and the Governments, State and Confederate; and whereas, it is right and proper that the wants of the army should be fully supplied, but lawfully done and not in a manner subversive of the rights of the citizens of this State, and that the mode of making impressments should be clearly defined and the rights both of the officer making the impressment and of the citizen whose property should or shall be impressed should be plainly made known—Therefore, *Preamble.*

SECTION 1. *Be it enacted by the Senate and House of Representatives of the State of Florida in General Assembly convened,* That any person or persons who shall in this State unlawfully impress or seize, under color of military authority, any goods, provisions, or other productions, or any property whatever, shall be guilty of a misdemeanor, and, upon conviction thereof, shall be imprisoned for a period of not less than one year, nor more than five years, at the discretion of the Court. *Unlawful impressment.* *Penalty.*

SEC. 2. *Be it further enacted,* That any person or persons who shall be aggrieved by any impressing officer in this State, or any agent of said officer, or any person claiming to have authority to act as such, by any unlawful impressment, shall have a remedy against such person or persons by petition, filed by himself or his agent or attorney *de facto* before any Circuit Court Judge, at Chambers or in open Court, and, immediately upon the filing of said petition with the Judge, he shall issue an order directing the defendant to appear before said Judge, at such time and places he may designate therein, and then and there to defend said suit, or judgment will be entered and rendered against him on default thereof, and said order shall be returnable instanter; and upon the appearance of the defendant, as in said order directed, or upon default thereof if the order is returned, the Judge shall proceed to try said cause, and shall cause the Sheriff to summon a jury of twelve citizens of the county to try said cause, and the Judge shall proceed with this cause and try the same forthwith and render such judgment as the law and facts demand and the jury find, and cause execution to issue instanter against the *Penalty of persons aggrieved by unlawful impressment.*

5

lands and tenements, goods and chattels and slaves of the defendant; and said execution shall be levied and collected by the Sheriff, and said Sheriff shall levy on and sell the property of the defendant as in other cases of Sheriff's sale: *Provided, however,* That notice of said sale shall be given by posting in three public places for ten days, and no stay law or other law shall prevent the sale from being made in ten days, nor shall any replevin or forthcoming bond be allowed; and the Sheriff and Clerk of the Circuit Courts shall execute all orders of the Judge under this act: *Provided, however,* That the same proceedings may be had before any two Justices of the Peace in this State, and they shall have the same civil power and jurisdiction as the Judges of the Circuit Court under this act; and whenever any petition as aforesaid is brought before any two Justices of Peace, the Sheriff and Clerk of the Circuit Court of the county where the petition is brought shall attend upon said special Justices' Court, and shall obey all orders of the said Justices of the Peace under this act; and no form of written pleadings shall be required under this act.

List of officers authorized to impress.

SEC. 3. *Be it further enacted,* That the Governor shall cause a list to be made of all persons or officers who are authorized to make impressments in this State for the use of the Confederate Government, which list he shall cause to be published in some newspaper in this State and in three public places in each county.

Proclamation by Governor.

SEC. 4. *Be it further enacted,* That the Governor shall issue a proclamation, calling upon all citizens to furnish all their surplus provisions for the use of the army of the Confederate States, in order that all necessity for impressment may cease and the country preserved from the inconvenience and injury of the State and its citizens; and in said proclamation inform the public who are authorized to impress, and no others shall be authorized to impress in this State than those persons whose names are reported to the Governor and published by him in proclamation.

Persons authorized to impress.

SEC. 5. *Be it further enacted,* That each and every person authorized by Confederate authority or law of the Confederate States to make impressments in this State, shall notify the Governor thereof, so that the citizens of this State may be notified thereof by proclamation of the Governor as aforesaid.

Officers attempting to impress unlawfully.

SEC. 6. *Be it further enacted,* That if any Confederate officer shall impress, or attempt to impress, or order impressed, any provisions in this State by force, contrary to the provisions of this act or the impressment act of Congress, it shall be the duty of the Governor of this State to demand of the President of the Confederate States the immediate removal from this State of such officer or officers.

Provisions on way to market.

SEC. 7. *Be it further enacted,* That no provisions shall be impressed in this State while in market, or on the way to the same, for the purpose of sale in such market: *Provided, however,* That the owner of such property shall be allowed five days to expose said goods or property in market, and that the words "on the way to the same" shall be construed to mean such reasonable time as may be necessary to reach said market, or the place where he proposes to sell them, to supply the inhabitants of this State.

Passed the Senate November 23, 1863. Passed the House of Representatives December 1, 1863. Approved by the Governor December 3, 1863.

CHAPTER 1,415—[No. 32.]

AN ACT to aid the Confederate Government in the detection of Frauds.

WHEREAS, It is the duty of the citizens and authorities of each State to guard and protect the character and welfare of the Confederate States of America; and, whereas, the Congress of the Confederate States of America, by an act approved May 1st, 1863, passed an act entitled " an act to prevent fraud in the Quarter-Master's and Commissary's Departments, and the obtaining under false pretence transportation for private property," among the provisions of which appear the following, to-wit: *Preamble.*

SEC. 2. That no officer charged with the safe keeping, transfer or disbursement of public moneys, or charged with or assigned to the duty of purchasing for the government, or any department thereof, shall buy, trade, traffic or speculate in either, directly or indirectly, for the purpose of gain to himself or other, by re-sale or otherwise, any article of food, or clothing, or material of which the same is made, or which enter into or constitutes a part of the same, or any material of war or article whatsoever which is or may be required to be purchased for the use of the army or the prosecution of the war.

SEC. 3. No officer shall take a receipt in blank for any article or articles purchased by him for the government or any department thereof; and every receipt shall set forth the true amount paid, and on what account; and when payment is made on account of property purchased, the receipt shall set forth the name of the person from whom such property was purchased and the place of his residence, the thing or things purchased by items, numbers, weight or measurement, as may be customary in the particular case, the price thereof and the date of payment.

SEC. 4. No officer who is in charge of transportation, or who is empowered to grant the same, shall forward by government conveyance, or at the expense of government, or to the exclusion or delay of government freight, any commodity or property of any

1863.

kind, unless the same belongs to the government or some department thereof, except as authorized by law. Therefore, in order to aid the Confederate Government in the discovery of violations of the act herein recited, and in punishing the offenders,

SECTION 1. *Be it enacted by the Senate and House of Representatives of the State of Florida in General Assembly convened,* That it shall be the duty of the Judge of Probate in each county of the State to advertise from time to time for information, and to take the testimony in writing, under oaths, of any respectable white person or persons of any transaction of fraudulent character which has heretofore been practiced or attempted to be practiced, or shall hereafter be practiced or attempted to be practiced, by any officer or agent of the Confederate Government, and for this purpose he is hereby authorized to have summoned and compel the attendance of any witness or witnesses, and the evidence so taken by him he shall certify under the seal of the Court, specifying the name of the officer or agent and all others concerned with him, and forward the same to the Governor of the State.

Judges of Probate to advertise for information.

SEC. 2. *Be it further enacted,* That it shall be the duty of the Governor and he is hereby required to record, or have recorded, in a book to be provided for that purpose, and to be kept in the Executive Department, the evidence or statements he may receive and to forward the said evidence or statements to the proper department of the Confederate Government.

Governor to have evidence recorded.

Passed the Senate November 26, 1863. Passed the House of Representatives December 1, 1863. Approved by the Governor December 3, 1863.

CHAPTER 1,416—[No. 33.]

AN ACT to be entitled an act to amend the election laws of this State relative to soldiers voting.

SECTION 1. *Be it enacted by the Senate and House of Representatives of the State of Florida in General Assembly convened,* That in all elections for members of Congress from this State, or any member of the Senate or House of Representatives of this State, if the officer highest in command of any troops from this State, whether the same be in this State or not, does not order an election in the camp or post under his command, on the day of election fixed by law, then it shall and may be lawful for all qualified voters from this State under command of such officer so neglecting to order an election, to assemble themselves and their votes under the superintendence of any three qualified voters of their command, who are hereby authorized to swear each other in as managers of such election.

Officer in command failing to order election.

SEC. 2. *Be it further enacted*, That it shall be the duty of said managers to forward by mail or otherwise such election returns to the Judge of Probate of the County of the person or persons voted for as a member or members to the House of Representatives of this State, and to the Secretary of State of this State for all persons voted for as Senator or member to Congress.

SEC. 3. *Be it further enacted*, That in all cases where such soldiers are on detail or other service out of the camp or post to which they belong, in numbers of three or more persons together, that it shall and may be lawful for them to cast their vote under the superintendence of any three of their number, as provided in the first section of this act, who shall make return of the same as provided for in the second section of this act; and in no case shall said returns be rejected for want of form.

SEC. 4. *Be it further enacted*, That said votes shall be canvassed by the Board of County Canvassers on the twentieth day after any such election, and certified by them in the same manner as now provided by law in the canvass of other election returns in military camps.

Passed the Senate November 27, 1863. Passed the House of Representatives December 2, 1863. Approved by the Governor December 3, 1863.

CHAPTER 1,417—[No. 34.]

AN ACT in relation to forfeited bonds of criminals.

SECTION 1. *Be it enacted by the Senate and House of Representatives of the State of Florida in General Assembly convened*, That whenever any bond or recognizance has been taken for the appearance of any person before any Court in this State charged with a criminal offence, and he fails to appear or give his attendance in conformity with said bond or recognizance, the Clerk of the Circuit Court shall issue a *scire facias* against the principal and sureties, to show cause at the next term of the Circuit Court why judgment should not be entered up and execution issue for the penalty thereof.

SEC. 2. *Be it further enacted*, That the matter shall then be submitted to the Court and jury for their adjudication without further pleadings.

SEC. 3. *Be it further enacted*, That in case any of the signers to the bond or recognizance should be beyond the jurisdiction of the Court for service, then he or they shall be made parties by publication in some newspaper published within the State for three months.

Passed the Senate November 21, 1863. Passed the House of Representatives December 2, 1863. Approved by the Governor December 3, 1863.

CHAPTER 1,418—[No. 35.]

AN ACT to be entitled an act to legalize the acts of Samuel Lowe, acting Clerk of the Circuit Court.

SECTION 1. *Be it enacted by the Senate and House of Repre sentatives of the State of Florida in General Assembly convened,* That the acts of Samuel Lowe, while performing the duties of Deputy Clerk in and for the County of Duval, be and are hereby declared valid to all intent and purposes though said Lowe had been actually Clerk of the Circuit Court for said county.

Passed the Senate November 30, 1863. Passed the House of Representatives December 1, 1863. Approved by the Governor December 3, 1863.

CHAPTER 1,419—[No. 36.]

AN ACT to provide for the payment for Plats furnished the counties of Clay, Jackson and Calhoun.

Register to be paid for plats.

SECTION 1. *Be it enacted by the Senate and House of Repre sentatives of the State of Florida in General Assembly convened,* That the Register of Public Lands shall receive for preparing, or causing to be prepared, for the counties of Clay, Jackson and Calhoun, township plats of the lands embraced therein and lists showing the dates of entries and names of purchasers, as required by resolution requiring plats of the Public Lands to be furnished the various counties, approved December 15, 1862, five dollars for each township embraced in said counties, to be paid by the Treasurer upon the warrant of the Comptroller.

Repeal.

SEC. 2. *Be it further enacted,* That the resolution requiring plats of the public lands to be furnished the various counties, approved December 15, 1862, be and the same is hereby repealed.

Passed the Senate November 26, 1863. Passed the House of Representatives December 3, 1863. Approved by the Governor December 3, 1863.

CHAPTER 1,420—[No. 37.]

AN ACT to provide for the relief of Soldiers' Families and others that require assistance.

SECTION 1. *Be it enacted by the Senate and House of Repre sentatives of the State of Florida in General Assembly convened,*

That the sum of five hundred thousand dollars be and the same is hereby appropriated, out of any moneys in the Treasury not otherwise appropriated, to be applied to the relief of the families **Appropriation.** of such soldiers as are now in the military service of this State or of the Confederate States, or who may hereafter be in the service of this State or of the Confederate States, or who have **Persons to be** died, were wounded, or became disabled by sickness or wounds **relieved.** while in said service, and of all soldiers who were wounded or disabled by sickness while in either of said service, and all mothers, fathers, sisters and brothers who have sons or brothers in either of said service, or who were wounded or otherwise disabled by either of said service, or who have died while in either of said service, and who require assistance in this State: *Provi-* **Proviso.** *ded, however,* The family of no soldier who is a deserter from his command shall be entitled to assistance under this act.

SEC. 2. *Be it further enacted,* That to assist in carrying out the purposes of this act, the Governor is hereby authorized to issue Treasury Notes to the amount of three hundred thousand **Issue of Treasu-** dollars, to be issued in the same manner as is now provided by **ry Notes.** law for the issue of Treasury Notes, or so much thereof as he may deem necessary.

SEC. 3. *Be it further enacted,* That it shall be the duty of the County Commissioners, assisted by the Justices of the Peace in the several counties in this State, to prepare a list of the families **List of families.** in the first section of this act who actually require assistance, stating those that are needy and those that are most needy, seting forth in said list the name of the soldier and the name of each member of his family to whom said aid is to be given, and their respective ages; and County Commissioners and Judges of Probate shall consolidate and prepare a list, to be kept in the Judge of Probate's office, and forward a certified copy thereof to the Comptroller of this State as soon as said list can possibly be prepared, after the approval of this act; and a corrected list of the same shall be forwarded by the first day of June next thereafter.

SEC. 4. *Be it further enacted,* That the Governor cause the distribution of the monies herein appropriated to be made semi-annually, first, as soon after the approval of this act as practicable; **Distribution of** and second, by the first day of August next thereafter, or as near **monies to be** that time as conveniently may be for the use of the soldiers and **made by Gov'r.** families herein provided for, according to the necessities of the several counties in this State, being governed by the list on file in the Comptroller's office, and by his knowledge of their several necessities, the prices of provisions, clothing and supplies; and the Governor shall draw his order upon the Comptroller for said amounts, and said Comptroller shall issue his warrant for the same in favor of the County Commissioners of the several counties, for the support of soldiers or soldiers' families, as provided for in this act; and the Treasurer shall pay the same to the Judge

1863.

of Probate or his order, or the Trustees hereinafter provided for or their order.

SEC. 5. *Be it further enacted,* That whenever there is no Board of County Commissioners in any county, or where such Board fail or refuse to perform the duties by this act enjoined, the Governor shall appoint suitable persons to perform the duties herein required of the County Commissioners and Judge of Probate; and the Comptroller shall issue his warrant, inserting their names as Trustees of the county for the purposes aforesaid.

Gov'r may appoint agents.

SEC. 6. *Be it further enacted,* That the money so paid out of the Treasury shall be expended by the Board of County Commissioners or by the Board of Trustees of the county, appointed as aforesaid, in clothing, provisions, cards, spinning wheels and necessary family supplies for such persons as hereinbefore mentioned, and shall cause the same to be faithfully, justly and equitably distributed, or shall pay said soldier or soldiers' family, or other persons, as heretofore provided for, his, her or their *pro rata* share of said money, at the discretion of the Judge of Probate or Trustees.

Money how to be expended.

SEC. 7. *Be it further enacted,* That in making out the list of the different families, the County Commissioners or Trustees, as aforesaid appointed, shall enumerate with those who are to receive aid those who have left the county on account of invasion by the enemy, but who intend returning as soon as the said invasion shall cease; they shall be also authorized and empowered to add to the list such person or persons as are provided for in this act; also to erase the names of such person or persons who are, in their judgment, not entitled to the provisions of this act, and to send such amended list to the Comptroller of this State as soon as is practicable, after the approval of this act, and by the first day of June next thereafter, for the purpose of their receiving the said aid as is intended by the provisions of this act.

Manner of preparing lists.

SEC. 8. *Be it further enacted,* That the Governor be and he is hereby authorized to cause to be drawn from the Treasury, by warrant of the Comptroller, in favor of the several Judges of Probate or Trustees appointed as aforesaid, or their respective orders, such portion of the money herein appropriated as may, in his judgment, be adequate and necessary to supply and meet the immediate wants of the soldiers and families provided for in this act, being governed in making such advance by the respective lists as have heretofore been forwarded to the Comptroller by the several Judges of Probate of this State, and the inability to provide for their support and the prices of provisions, clothing, and other articles necessary to the support of said families in such county.

Governor to advance funds.

SEC. 9. *Be it further enacted,* That the Judges of Probate and County Commissioners of the several counties, in the distribution of the monies received under the provisions of this act, are

Manner of distribution.

hereby required to distribute the same to soldiers, soldiers' families and others hereinbefore specified, according to his, her or their actual situation, means of support and ability of supporting themselves, discriminating between the needy and the most needy.

SEC. 10. *Be it further enacted*, That the Governor shall cause five hundred copies of this act to be printed immediately after his approval of the same, and said copies shall be distributed amongst the members of the General Assembly for the purpose of distribution in the several counties.

Copies of acts to be printed.

SEC. 11. *Be it further enacted*, That the Governor be and he is hereby authorized and requested to contract for and purchase three thousand pairs of cotton cards and five hundred pairs of wool cards for the aid of persons who are provided for in this act, and to cause the same to be distributed among the several counties for distribution to the poor; and the Governor shall issue his order on the Treasurer for the money necessary to purchase said cards, and the Comptroller shall issue his warrant for the same, and the Treasurer shall pay the same; and there is hereby appropriated a sufficient sum, in addition to the appropriation hereinbefore made, to pay for the same out of any money in the Treasury not otherwise appropriated.

Cotton cards.

SEC. 12. *Be it further enacted*, That the County Commissioners of the several counties in this State be, and they are hereby authorized to levy, assess and collect a tax sufficient to meet the necessities of the persons provided for in this act in their respective counties.

County tax.

SEC. 13. *Be it further enacted*, That the Governor be and he is hereby authorized to send to the several Judges of Probate, or Trustees of the counties, the amount to which they may be entitled by any person whom he may consider trustworthy.

Passed the Senate November 30, 1863. Passed the House of Representatives December 2, 1863. Approved by the Governor December 3, 1863.

CHAPTER 1,421—[No. 38.]

AN ACT to appropriate ten thousand dollars for the Wayside Homes or Hospitals in this State.

SECTION 1. *Be it enacted by the Senate and House of Representatives of the State of Florida in General Assembly convened*, That the sum of ten thousand dollars, or so much of the same as the Governor may deem necessary, be and it is hereby placed at

Appropriation.

6

the disposal of the Governor, to afford aid and assistance to the
Wayside Homes or Hospitals in this State, established to aid and
assist the soldiers of the Confederate States, and that the Comptroller issue his warrant on the order of the Governor to the
Treasurer, and the Treasurer shall pay the same.

Passed the Senate December 3, 1863. Passed the House of Representatives
December 3, 1863. Approved by the Governor December 3, 1863.

CHAPTER 1,422—[No. 39.]

AN ACT to prevent and punish all persons Planting and Cultivating, in the
State of Florida, over a certain quantity of land in Cotton and Tobacco during
the continuance of the present war.

SECTION 1. *Be it enacted by the Senate and House of Representatives of the State of Florida in General Assembly convened,*
That from and after the passage of this act, it shall not be law-
Prohibiting cot- ful for any person or persons, whether residing in this State or
ton.
not, to plant and cultivate, in any county in this State, by themselves, agents or employees, or allow the same to be done, a great-
Hands.
er number of acres of land in cotton than one acre for each hand
owned or employed by them between the ages of fifteen and
sixty, and when said persons may own or employ hands over sixty
years of age and under seventy, and over nine and under fifteen,
two of said hands shall be counted as one hand ; therefore said
person or persons may plant and cultivate one acre of land in
cotton, and no more, for every two of said hands so owned and
employed by them.

SEC. 2. *Be it further enacted,* That any person or persons
whatever violating the provisions of this act, shall be guilty of a
Penalty.
misdemeanor, and upon conviction thereof, shall be fined for every acre so planted, more than one acre to the hand, and so on
in proportion to the number of hands employed, the sum of one
thousand dollars for each and every acre so planted above the
number specified, one-half of which sum shall be, in case where
there is a prosecutor or informer, paid to said prosecutor and
Informer.
informer, the other half paid to the County Commissioners of
the County where the misdemeanor is committed, for the benefit
of indigent soldiers' families in said county.

SEC. 3. *Be it further enacted,* That any person or persons who
may intend or desire to prosecute any person or persons for the
violation of this act, may, upon application to any Justice of the
Peace of said county, supported by affidavit that he has good
reasons to believe that the provisions of this act have been viola-
Surveyor.
ted, obtain an order requiring the County Surveyor, or where

there is no County Surveyor, any other competent Surveyor, to enter the premises and make a survey of all lands so planted and cultivated in cotton ; and said person shall pay said Surveyor for making said survey his usual fees, which shall be taxed in the bill of costs on the final adjudication of the same.

SEC. 4. *Be it further enacted*, That all owners or employees of slaves shall give in to the Tax Receiver the number of hands owned and employed by them between the ages of nine and fifteen, and fifteen and sixty, and sixty and seventy, each year during the present war.

SEC. 5. *Be it further enacted*, That no owner, or owners, or employers of slaves in this State, shall plant more than one-quarter of an acre of land in Tobacco to the hand, and any person so offending shall be guilty of a misdemeanor, and, upon conviction, be subject to the penalties of the foregoing section of this act.

SEC. 6. *Be it further enacted*, That all persons who will manufacture, themselves, all of the cotton they may make, to be sold to the people of this State, at or below the amount fixed by the Commissioners of this State, under the laws of the Confederate States, or to be woven by them and used in clothing their families and negroes, are hereby declared exempt from the operations of this law : *Provided*, That this section shall be so construed as to mean that persons can only cultivate any amount of cotton they see fit for their own manufactories, or to be woven and used by them as aforesaid, and to be sold to the people of this State at the aforesaid rates.

SEC. 7. *Be it further enacted*, That the Judges of the Circuit Courts of this State are hereby required to give this law in special charge to the Grand Juries at each term of their Courts during the existence of the present war.

SEC. 8. *Be it further enacted*, That the Governor shall cause this act to be published in the several papers of this State immediately after his approval of the same.

SEC. 9. *Be it further enacted*, That the provisions of this act shall be in full force and effect during the continuance of the present war and no longer.

SEC. 10. *Be it further enacted*, That all laws conflicting with the provisions of this act be and the same are hereby repealed.

Passed the House of Representatives November 25, 1863. Passed the Senate December 1, 1863. Approved by the Governor December 3, 1863.

No. of hands.

Tobacco.

Manufacturers of cotton.

Judges to give this law in special charge.

Publication.

Limitation.

Repeal.

CHAPTER 1,423—[No. 40.]

AN ACT to prevent the distilling of Spirituous Liquors in this State.

SECTION 1. *Be it enacted by the Senate and House of Representatives of the State of Florida in General Assembly convened,* That from and after the passage of this act, it shall be unlawful for any person or persons to distil any spirituous liquor from any article of grain, sugar, molasses or syrup made from sugar cane or Chinese cane, potatoes, or from any other article or articles of subsistence, except the fruits of the country, or in any way or manner to create spirituous liquor from any of said articles ; and on conviction thereof, such person or persons shall be punished by fine not less than ten thousand dollars, and imprisoned for not less than one year nor more than two years, at the discretion of the Court.

Distilling prohibited.

SEC. 2. *Be it further enacted,* That it shall be the duty of the Governor, and he is hereby authorized and required to proceed forthwith, and in the most summary manner, to abate as a nuisance any distillery at work in this State contrary to the provisions of this act, and to cause the arrest and examination of any person or persons distilling as aforesaid, and to seize all liquor distilled contrary to the provisions of this act, and turn over the same to Hospital uses.

Gov'r to abate distilleries.

SEC. 3. *Be it further enacted,* That all licenses to distill spirituous liquors heretofore granted to persons in this State, by virtue of an act entitled an act to prevent the establishment of distilleries and the distilling of whiskey or other spirituous liquors, approved December 15th, 1862, shall cease, determine and be void from and after the passage of this act.

Licenses made void.

SEC. 4. *Be it further enacted,* That the third section of an act entitled an act to prevent the establishment of distilleries and the distilling of whiskey or other spirituous liquors be and it is hereby repealed, said act being approved December 15th, 1862.

Repeal.

SEC. 5. *Be it further enacted,* That the Governor shall issue his proclamation immediately after the passage of this act, and cause the same to be published in the newspapers of this State, and have copies thereof sent to the Sheriff of each county, notifying the public of the passage of this law.

Gov'r to issue proclamation.

SEC. 6. *Be it further enacted,* That if any Sheriff of this State shall fail or refuse to perform any duty required of him by the second section of this act, he shall, on conviction thereof, be fined and imprisoned at the discretion of the Court.

Sheriff to be fined and imprisoned.

SEC. 7. *Be it further enacted,* That the provisions of this act shall not apply to those who have a contract with the Confederate Government for the distilling of alcohol and are carrying out their contract in good faith, of which fact the Governor shall be

Contractor for distillation of Alcohol.

the judge: *And provided further*, That all distillers of alcohol in this State shall make quarterly returns to his Excellency the Governor, of the quantity distilled, to whom delivered, and accompanied with the receipt of the officer or officers in the State or Confederate States service.

SEC. 8. *Be it further enacted*, That the Governor shall issue a license to William H. Johnson, so that he may be enabled to execute and carry out his contract with the Confederate States.

License to Wm. H. Johnson.

Passed the House of Representatives November 30th, 1863. Passed the Senate December 1st, 1863. Approved by the Governor December 4th, 1863.

CHAPTER 1,424—[No. 41.]

AN ACT for the relief of Aaron W. DaCosta.

WHEREAS, By the provisions of an act of the General Assembly of Florida, entitled an act to amend the militia and patrol laws of this State, approved December 22nd, 1859, it was provided that all penalties and fines imposed by law under fifty dollars should be recovered by action of debt, in the name of the State of Florida, before any Justice of the Peace, and made it the duty of Captains of militia companies to institute suits in said Justices' Courts to recover the same: and whereas, numerous suits were instituted by Captains of companies in the Court of Aaron W. DaCosta, Esquire, a Justice of the Peace in and for the county of Duval, in conformity to said act, against defaulters for the recovery of the penalties and fines imposed by said act, in a very large number of which suits the defendants were found, upon trial, to be not subject to militia duty, or were found not guilty of offences against the militia laws of the State, or had paid the tax imposed by said act as an exemption from militia duty: and whereas, the costs that accrued and were due to said Justice could not be adjudged against said defendants, and have never been paid by the State, but are still due and owing.

Preamble.

SECTION 1. *Therefore be it enacted by the Senate and House of Representatives of the State of Florida in General Assembly convened*, That the Comptroller of Public Accounts be and he is hereby authorized to audit and allow to the said Aaron W. DaCosta, Esq., the amount of costs which shall be duly taxed and certified by him according to law, as due in said cases, and that the same be paid out of any monies in the Treasury not otherwise appropriated.

Comptroller to allow costs.

Passed the House of Representatives November 27, 1863. Passed the Senate November 30, 1863. Approved by the Governor December 3, 1863.

AN ACT further defining the duties of the Treasurer of the State.

SECTION 1. *Be it enacted by the Senate and House of Representatives of the State of Florida in General Assembly convened,*
That hereafter the Treasurer of the State shall not absent himself
from the State, or be absent himself from the Capitol, or from
the duties of his office, without the consent of the Governor in
writing, and under such limitations and restrictions as the Governor may impose.

*Treasurer may
not leave the
State.*

Passed the House of Representatives December 3, 1863. Passed the Senate
December 3, 1863. Approved by the Governor December 4, 1863.

CHAPTER 1,426—[No. 43.]

AN ACT to provide for furnishing to each Regiment and Battalion in Confederate service from this State a suitable Flag or Ensign, also a Flag to be used at the Capitol.

SECTION 1. *Be it enacted by the Senate and House of Representatives of the State of Florida in General Assembly convened,*
That the Governor be and he is hereby authorized and requested
to furnish to each regiment and battalion from this State in Confederate service a suitable Flag or Ensign in behalf of the State,
also a Flag of the Confederate States for the use of the State, to
be used at the Capitol, on suitable occasions, the expenses of procuring such Flags to be paid out of any money in the Treasury
not otherwise appropriated.

Flag to be furnished.

Passed the House of Representatives December 3, 1863. Passed the Senate
December 3, 1863. Approved by the Governor December 4, 1863.

CHAPTER 1,427—[No. 44.]

AN ACT to provide Clothing for Troops from Florida in the service of the Confederate States.

SECTION 1. *Be it enacted by the Senate and House of Representatives of the State of Florida in General Assembly convened,*
That an act entitled an act to authorize the Board of County
Commissioners of the several counties in this State to levy a

specific tax for the relief of the soldiers in the service of the State, or of the Confederate States, approved December 12, 1862, and an act entitled an act to amend an act entitled an act to authorize the Board of County Commissioners of the several counties of this State to levy a specific tax for the relief of the soldiers in the service of the State, or of the Confederate States, approved December 12, 1862, approved December 15, 1862, be and the same are hereby repealed.

Repeal.

SEC. 2. *Be it further enacted,* That the sum of seventy-five thousand dollars be and the same is hereby appropriated, out of any money in the Treasury not otherwise appropriated, to purchase the necessary materials for shoes and clothing, and to pay for having the same manufactured or made up into clothes, socks and shoes for the use of soldiers from Florida in the service of the Confederate States.

Appropriation.

SEC. 3. *Be it further enacted,* That the amount appropriated by the second section of this act shall be expended under the direction of the Governor and with the assistance of the Quarter-Master General of the State.

Gov'r to make expenditure.

Passed the House of Representatives November 28, 1863. Passed the Senate December 3, 1863. Approved by the Governor December 4, 1863.

CHAPTER 1,428—[No. 45.]

AN ACT making appropriations for the expenses of the Second Session of the Twelfth General Assembly, and for other purposes.

SECTION 1. *Be it enacted by the Senate and House of Representatives of the State of Florida in General Assembly convened,* That the following sums shall be paid out of any monies in the Treasury, not otherwise appropriated, to the following persons, to-wit: To E. J. Vann, President of the Senate, $163.20; James Abercrombie, 197.60; A. K. Allison, Senator, 19; J. M. Arnow, Senator, 137; J. P. Carter, Senator, 98.20; J. D. Clary, Senator, 135; J. C. Cooper, Senator, 245; D. P. Hogue, Senator, 165; D. P. Holland, Senator, 135; Edward Hopkins, Senator, 128; J. L. King, Senator, 112; Jesse Norwood, Senator, 195; W. C. Roper, Senator, 155; J. S. Russell, Senator, 101; T. T. Russell, Senator, 142.60; John Scott, Senator, 130; J. B. Smith, Senator, 161; J. M. Taylor, Senator, 159; —— Jones, Senator, 119; E. L. Cater, Senator, 197.60; J. B. Whitehurst, Secretary, 279; E. J. Judah, Assistant Secretary, 243; H. L. Howze, Engrossing Clerk, 190; E. M. West, Enrolling Clerk, 200; J. Brass, Recording Clerk, 250; J. White, Sergeant-at-Arms and Door-

Appropriation.

Senate.

Keeper, 300; R. E. Frier, 190. Thos. J. Eppes, Speaker of the House, 195; A. Richardson, Representative, 195; S. R. Sessions, Rep., 114; John F. Jackson, Rep., 145; W. B. Ross, Rep., 116; W. C. Newburn, Rep., 120; J. A. Lee, Rep., 140; G. W. Blackburn, Rep., 102.60; J. C. Greely, Rep., 140.40; R. T. H. Thomas, Rep., 145; T. J. McGehee, Rep., 113; A. Y. Hampton, Rep., 107; Neil Hendry, Rep., 113; T. Baltzell, Rep., 95; J. G. Smith, Rep., 115; F. R. Pittman, Rep., 195; W. B. Wynn, Rep., 110; F. Leslie, Rep., 75; O. M. Avery, Rep., 197.60; T. Hannah, Rep., 106.80; H. J. Seward, Rep., 175; N. T. Scott, Rep., 99; J. L. Campbell, Rep., 125; M. Hewett, Rep., 153; W. T. Duval, Rep., 195; A. Cromartie, Rep., 98.20; R. H. Bradford, Rep., 97.40; L. Dishong, Rep., 165; T. Y. Henry, Rep., 100; W. H. Gee, Rep., 100; Joseph Price, Rep., 117; I. V. Garnie, Rep., 131; A. J. Polhill, Rep., 110; T. J. W. Higginbotham, Rep., 135; J. Y. Jones, Rep., 91; E. M. Mattauer, Rep., 99; F. N. Foy, Rep., 145; H. Overstreet, Rep., 175; J. W. Price, Rep., 137; W. H. Arendell, Rep., 101; J. J. Williams, Rep., 95; J. P. Atkins, Rep. 76; David Mizell, Rep., 160; T. D. Nixon, Rep., 107; James M. Amos, Rep., 197.60; Thos. B. Barefoot, Clerk House, 264; W. F. Bynum, Assistant Clerk, 248; Thos. Williams, Engrossing Clerk, 190; W. M. McIntosh, Enrolling Clerk, 210; Oscar Hart, Assistant Enrolling Clerk, 80; F. M. Bunker, Recording Clerk, 250; G. W. Floyd, Sergeant-at-Arms, 195; J. J. Whitehurst, Messenger, 190; A. B. Campbell, Door-Keeper, 200; Rev. Ellis, Chaplain, 50.   For general print-

ing and publishing, to be audited by the Comptroller 9,000; printing Laws and Journal, to be audited by the Comptroller, in addition to the above 4,000.

SEC. 2. *Be it further enacted*, That the following sums be and the same are hereby appropriated for the fiscal year, 1864:

For salaries of public officers,	$33,600 00
For Jurors and State Witnesses,	20,000 00
Criminal Prosecutions and Contingent Expenses of the Circuit Court,	20,000 00
For Contingent Expenses of Supreme Court,	2,000 00
For interest on State Debt,	30,000 00
For maintenance of Lunatics,	15,000 00
For residence of Governor,	1,000 00
Post Mortem Examinations,	200 00
For Contingent Fund,	20,000 00
For Clerk hire for Executive,	1,500 00
For repairs of Capitol, to be audited by the Comptroller,	2,000 00
Appropriation for Stationery and Candles, to be purchased by order of Governor,	3,000 00
Incidental expenses of this General Assembly, to be audited by Comptroller,	400 00

Expenses preparing Treasury Notes for issue, Clerk
hire, &c.,................................... 15,000 00
Military purposes,............................ 25,000 00

Passed the House of Representatives December 3, 1863. Passed the Senate
December 3, 1863. Approved by the Governor December 4, 1863.

CHAPTER 1,429—[No. 46.]

AN ACT to amend an act to prevent the entry of lands occupied by Soldiers or
their Families during the continuance of the present war, and also to regulate
the entry and sale of Public Lands, approved Dec. 13th, 1862.

SECTION 1. *Be it enacted by the Senate and House of Representatives of the State of Florida in General Assembly convened,*
That the 8th section of the above recited act be and the same is
hereby so amended as to give to the legal heirs of the soldiers
referred to in said 8th section the right to perfect the title,
should the soldier die before the expiration of the two years
mentioned in said section.

Heirs of sol-
diers may enter
lands.

Passed the House of Representatives December 3, 1863. Passed the Senate
November 28, 1863. Approved by the Governor December 4, 1863.

7

RESOLUTIONS.

——o——

[No. 1.]

RESOLUTIONS of thanks to our Soldiers.

Be it resolved by the Senate and House of Representatives of the State of Florida in General Assembly convened, That the thanks of the State are due, and are hereby tendered through this legislative body, to the brave officers and soldiers of the State of Florida, for their gallant conduct in defence of her rights on many a well fought battle field.

Be it further resolved, That we do pledge ourselves, in honor and duty bound, to protect and maintain their families during their absence in the service of their country at any and every sacrifice.

Be it further resolved, That his Excellency the Governor be requested to forward a copy of these resolutions to each Florida brigade in the Confederate service, and to the commander in each district in this State; and that said commanders be requested by his Excellency the Governor, to have these resolutions read to the Florida troops under their commands.

Passed the Senate November 18, 1863. Passed the House of Representatives November 19, 1863. Approved by the Governor November 24, 1863.

———

[No. 2.]

RESOLUTION asking the Governor not to license any more Distilleries until the further action of the Legislature.

Be it resolved by the Senate and House of Representatives of the State of Florida in General Assembly convened, That the Governor be and he is hereby requested not to issue any more license to distillers for the distillation of spirituous liquors until the further action of the Legislature relative thereto.

Passed the House of Representatives November 20, 1863. Passed the Senate November 21, 1863. Approved by the Governor November 24, 1863.

[No. 3.]

RESOLUTIONS of thanks to Gen. Wm. Bailey and Dr. Henry Bacon..

Be it resolved by the Senate and House of Representatives of the State of Florida in General Assembly convened, That the gratitude of the people of this State is in an especial manner due Gen. Bailey, for the liberal and enlightened manner in which he is dispensing his means, and zeal and efficiency with which he supports the cause in which we are engaged.

Be it further resolved, That the thanks of the people of this State are eminently due Dr. Henry Bacon, a refugee from Georgia, for his known patriotism, hospitality, and in an especial manner for his generous donations to soldiers and soldiers' families in this State; and also to the Augusta Manufacturing Company, for the liberal aid afforded the said Dr. Bacon in carrying out his noble and patriotic purposes.

Be it further resolved, That his Excellency the Governor is hereby requested to cause a copy of the above resolutions to be forwarded to Gen. Bailey, Dr. Bacon and the Augusta Manufacturing Company.

Passed the House of Representatives November 19, 1863. Passed the Senate November 20, 1863. Approved by the Governor November 24, 1863.

[No. 4.]

RESOLUTIONS relating to the appointment of Agent for Soldiers' Families in the counties of Santa Rosa and Escambia.

Be it resolved by the Senate and House of Representatives of the State of Florida in General Assembly convened, That the Governor be and he is hereby authorized to appoint an Agent for the purpose of purchasing supplies for the families of soldiers in the counties of Escambia and Santa Rosa.

Agent to be appointed.

Resolved 2nd. That the person so appointed shall in no case have a claim against the State for any service he may render, or for any expense he may incur under this appointment.

Resolved 3rd. That no person shall be appointed by the Governor without satisfactory evidence that the person appointed is exempt from conscription under the acts of Congress, the Governor to be judge of the sufficiency of the evidence.

Passed the House of Representatives November 20, 1863. Passed the Senate November 23, 1863. Approved by the Governor November 25, 1863.

[No. 5.]

RESOLUTION relative to Tax in Kind.

WHEREAS, Neither justice nor necessity requires that the poor women of the country, whose husbands and sons are in the service, should be oppressed with a tax upon the produce raised by their personal exertions—Therefore,

Be it resolved by the Senate and House of Representatives of the State of Florida in General Assembly convened, That our Senators and Representatives in Congress be instructed and requested to use their best endeavors to have the present law, providing for a Tax in Kind, so amended as to exempt from the operations of said law all women in the possession of farms whose husbands or sons are in the service, and who have no slaves.

Be it further resolved, That the Governor be requested to transmit a copy of these resolutions to each of our Senators and Representatives in Congress.

Passed the House of Representatives November 24, 1863. Passed the Senate November 24, 1863. Approved by the Governor, November 30, 1863.

Preamble.

Representativ's in Congress requested.

[No. 6.]

RESOLUTION setting apart a Day of Fasting, Humiliation and Prayer

Be it resolved by the Senate and House of Representatives of the State of Florida in General Assembly convened, That the 24th day of December next be set apart throughout the State as a day of Fasting, Humiliation and Prayer, and that His Excellency, the Governor, is hereby requested to issue his proclamation to that effect.

Passed the Senate November 28, 1863. Passed the House of Representatives December 1, 1863. Approved by the Governor December 2, 1863.

[No. 7.]

JOINT RESOLUTION relative to our sick or wounded Soldiers in Gen. Bragg's army.

Be it resolved by the Senate and House of Representatives of the State of Florida in General Assembly convened, That the

1863.

Governor to ap-
point agents.

Governor do, without delay, appoint such number of energetic, prudent and humane citizens as may be necessary, and send them to the army of Gen. Bragg, to afford all the aid and assistance they can, and provide for the comfort and care of the soldiers from Florida in said army, and to attend to their wants and comfort ; and there is hereby placed at the disposal of the Governor the sum of twenty-five thousand dollars for that purpose, which shall be drawn by warrant of the Comptroller upon the order of the Governor, and the Treasurer shall pay the same.

Passed the Senate December 1, 1863. Passed the House of Representatives December 1, 1863. Approved by the Governor December 3, 1863.

[No. 8.]

RESOLUTION for the destruction of the State Bonds on hand of the issues of 1856 and 1861.

Be it resolved by the Senate and House of Representatives of the State of Florida in General Assembly convened, That the Committee on Finances and the Comptroller be and the same are hereby authorized and required to receive from the Treasurer the $206,000 of State Bonds of 1856, which were formerly hypothecated, and the $2,500 of the issue of 1861, which were returned from Richmond as informal, and cause the same to be destroyed by fire, the Comptroller to endorse said destruction upon his record of each bond, with the number of coupons and the date.

Bonds to be de-
stroyed.

Passed the House of Representatives November 30, 1863. Passed the Senate December 1, 1863. Approved by the Governor December 3, 1863.

[No. 9.]

RESOLUTIONS relative to Confederate Treasury Notes.

Preamble.

WHEREAS, It has been made known to this General Assembly, that certain citizens in this State, not having the welfare of the country at heart, but selfishly and meanly designing to discredit the public currency, and oppress their fellow-citizens by refusing to receive Confederate Treasury Notes in payment of debts or for the purchase of the necessaries of life, thereby acting in a manner which, if commonly pursued, would ruin the finances of our Government and eventually subvert our liberties—Therefore,

Be it resolved by the Senate and House of Representatives of the State of Florida in General Assembly convened, That the refusal to receive Confederate currency and all intentional attempts to discredit and depreciate the same, is conduct unworthy of a citizen of this State, and we denounce the same as hostile to the dearest rights, interests and liberties of our country. That as the whole fabric of our social and political existence depends on the maintenance of the Confederate cause, and that cause cannot be sustained without means and resources, therefore we regard any citizen who discredits and pursues such a course as will depreciate and destroy the Confederate currency as acting with the enemies of our country and unworthy the confidence, countenance or toleration of his fellow-citizens, if not a traitor to the country.

Resolved, That if any person shall refuse to receive Confederate currency in this State, who holds any position that exempts him from military service, the fact should be at once brought to the attention of the authorities, and such person placed immediately in the service.

Passed the House of Representatives December 4, 1863. Passed the Senate December 2, 1863. Approved by the Governor December 3, 1863.

Resolution.

Persons refusing to receive Confederate currency.

Persons exempt from military service.

[No. 10.]

RESOLUTION relative to the civil authority of the State of Florida.

WHEREAS, The principles of civil liberty transmitted to us by our fathers are of a paramount importance to the people of this State, and are consecrated to us not only by our own experience of their dignity and worth, but by the approval of the great and wise men who stand pre-eminent in the admiration and esteem of mankind, and that the continued inculcation of these precepts is highly important to us as the citizens of a sovereignty—Therefore,

Be it resolved by the Senate and House of Representatives of the State of Florida in General Assembly convened, That the civil authority is the supreme and paramount power in this State, to which the military authority is in all cases strictly and absolutely subordinate. That all laws, both civil and military, derive their just and only wise interpretation through the judicial tribunals of the State and Confederate Governments, each acting in their own prescribed spheres. That the General Assembly of

Preamble.

Resolution.

Civil authority supreme.

1863.

this State, while deeply sensible of its obligations to the Confederate Government, recognize no power or authority supreme over it in the discharge of its lawful and recognized duties in the making of such laws as are necessary for the well being and protection of the people of the State of Florida. That this General Assembly, in the name of the people of the State of Florida and of their sovereignty, expresses its profound disapproval and censure of all officers in the military service who are forgetful that the tenure of their authority is derived from the will of the people, expressed through the forms of civil law, and will tolerate no assumption of arbitrary authority within her limits.

Passed the House of Representatives November 25, 1863. Passed the Senate November 30, 1863. Approved by the Governor December 3, 1863.

[No. 11.]

JOINT RESOLUTION authorizing the Joint Committee on Finance and Public Accounts to destroy a sum of money therein named.

Treasury notes redeemed.

Be it resolved by the Senate and House of Representatives of the State of Florida in General Assembly convened, That the Joint Committee of the Senate and House on Finance and Public Accounts be instructed to destroy by fire the sum of forty-eight thousand four hundred and thirty-nine dollars and fifty-five cents, redeemed under Ordinance 49, and now in the Treasurer's office.

Passed the Senate December 3, 1863. Passed the House of Representatives December 3, 1863. Approved by the Governor December 3, 1863.

[No. 12.]

JOINT RESOLUTION relative to the Arsenal.

Governor to take control of Arsenal.

Be it resolved by the Senate and House of Representatives of the State of Florida in General Assembly convened, That the Governor is hereby directed to take the Arsenal under his control and custody, and have the same safely kept, and he is hereby authorized to appoint D. P. Holland to take charge of the same under his orders : *Provided, however,* The said D. P. Holland shall give his services to the Governor gratis, and shall have no charge or allowance for the same : *And provided further,* That the Governor may allow the Confederate States to store property therein.

Passed the Senate December 3, 1863. Passed the House of Representatives December 3, 1863. Approved by the Governor December 3, 1863.

. [No. 13.]

JOINT RESOLUTION in relation to the unsettled accounts of Ex-Gov. M. S. Perry, Quarter Master General H. V. Snell, and John W. Pearson, Disbursing Agent.

Be it resolved by the Senate and House of Representatives of the State of Florida in General Assembly convened, That the Governor shall appoint an accountant, to be confirmed by the Senate at this session, whose duty it shall be to settle the accounts of Ex-Gov. M. S. Perry, Quarter Master General H. V. Snell and John W. Pearson, disbursing agent, and said accountant shall have full power to settle said accounts between each and every of said persons and the State of Florida, and between each of themselves and each other ; and the Comptroller shall settle the same upon the exhibit and report of the said accountant, and shall issue his warrant on the sums found due by the accountant, or charge the person with the indebtedness found due by the accountant ; and the Treasurer shall pay on the warrant of the Comptroller, and the Comptroller shall issue his warrant on the accountant's balance, and said accountant shall make report to the next General Assembly ; and that the expenses of said accountant shall be equally divided between the State of Florida and each of said persons, and said accountant shall, before entering on his office, be sworn to honestly and faithfully perform and discharge the duties herein imposed on him.

Accountant to be appointed.

Balance due.

Passed the Senate December 2, 1863. Passed the House of Representatives December 3, 1863. Approved by the Governor December 3, 1863.

[No. 14.]

RESOLUTION in relation to the accounts of the late United States Receivers and Registers.

Be it resolved by the Senate and House of Representatives of

8

1863.

Salaries of U.
S. Receivers &
Registers.

the *State of Florida in General Assembly convened,* That in settling the accounts of the late Receiver and Registers of the United States Land Offices in this State, the Register of Public Lands be and he is hereby authorized to allow to said Receivers and Registers the salary that would have been due to them under the laws of the United States up to the time when the books, documents and other property belonging to their several offices were delivered and transferred to the Register of Public Lands upon his requisition.

Passed the Senate December 3, 1863. Passed the House of Representatives December 3, 1863. Approved by the Governor December 4, 1863.

[No. 15.]

RESOLUTION in relation to copying the Laws.

Governor to
employ copyist.

Be it resolved by the Senate and House of Representatives of the State of Florida in General Assembly convened, That the Governor be authorized to employ some suitable and competent person to copy the laws passed at this session of the General Assembly, and the sum of one hundred and twenty-five dollars be hereby appropriated for said services.

Passed the House of Representatives December 3, 1863. Passed the Senate December 3, 1863. Approved by the Governor December 4, 1863.

[No. 16.]

JOINT RESOLUTION relative to the pay of the Soldiers of the Confederate States.

Pay of soldiers.

Be it resolved by the Senate and House of Representatives of the State of Florida in General Assembly convened, That our Senators and Representatives in Congress be requested to use their best endeavors to cause the pay of the soldiers in the Confederate States Army to be raised and increased by such legislation as in their judgment will best conduce to that end.

Passed the Senate December 3, 1863. Passed the House of Representatives December 3, 1863. Approved by the Governor December 4, 1863.

[No. 17.]

JOINT RESOLUTION in relation to exempting the Workmen and persons employed in the Jefferson Manufacturing Company.

Resolved, That if any amendment to the present law of Congress exempting certain persons from military service be designed or adopted by Congress, that our Senators and Representatives in Congress be and they are hereby requested to use their endeavors to have exempted the workmen and persons employed in the Jefferson Manufacturing Company, their services being indespensable in conducting this useful and important work.

Resolved, That the Governor be and he is hereby requested to forward a copy of these resolutions to our representatives in Congress.

Passed the House of Representatives December 3, 1863. Passed the Senate December 3, 1863. Approved by the Governor December 4, 1863.

[No. 18.]

RESOLUTION in reference to exportation and importation of certain articles by private enterprise.

WHEREAS, The exportation of cotton, tobacco and other products from the Confederate States by private enterprise, and for private emoluments, tend to depreciate the currency, to corrupt public morals, to lessen the production of food and otherwise to injure the cause for which we are fighting, *Preamble.*

Be it therefore resolved by the Senate and House of Representatives of the State of Florida in General Assembly convened, That our Senators and Representatives in Congress be requested *Resolutions.* to inquire into the expediency of causing such legislation as will prevent all commercial intercourse with foreign counties not recognizing us, except by and for the benefit of the Confederate or State Government.

Be it further resolved, That our Senators and Representatives in Congress use their best endeavors to have the importation of foreign goods from foreign countries prevented by law, except on account of the State or of the Confederate States.

Passed the House of Representatives December 2, 1863. Passed the Senate December 3, 1863. Approved by the Governor December 4, 1863.

[No. 19.]

RESOLUTIONS relative to appointment of Agents in Greenville and Montgomery.

Be it resolved by the Senate and House of Representatives of the State of Florida in General Assembly convened, That the Governor be and he is hereby authorized to appoint two agents to receive and disburse the fund appropriated for the relief of soldiers' families who may reside on or near the line of the Ala. & Fla. Railroad, of Ala., one of said agents to be a resident of Greenville, Ala., the other to reside in the city of Montgomery, Ala.

Governor to appoint agents.

Resolved 2nd, That these agents are to receive no pay or emoluments whatever, from either the State or the beneficiaries of the fund, but are to be selected from those who are willing to perform the duties required from regard to the great cause in which we are all engaged.

Agents to receive no pay.

Passed the House of Representatives December 3, 1863. Passed the Senate December 3, 1863. Approved by the Governor December 4, 1863.

[No. 20.]

RESOLUTION in relation to the war between the Confederate States and the United States.

WHEREAS,The State of Florida, by her Convention, in severing the political ties that bound her to the old Union, pledged her last dime and last man to the support of our cause for independence; And, whereas, the last General Assembly declared that Florida, one of the first States to secede from the old Union, will be one of the last to lay down arms, " and in the impending struggle for our lives and liberties " will stand by her sister States to the last man and last musket, until peace is established on the basis of a separate nationality and the independence of the Confederate States unconditionally acknowledged by the United States—Therefore,

Preamble.

Be it resolved by the Senate and House of Representatives of the State of Florida in General Assembly convened, That it is the sense of this General Assembly that these pledges should be redeemed at all hazards.

Resolution.

Passed the Senate December 3, 1863. Passed the House of Representatives December 4, 1863. Approved by the Governor December 4, 1863.

INDEX

TO THE

ACTS AND RESOLUTIONS

. OF THE

Second Session of the Twelfth General Assembly.

ADMINISTRATORS AND EXECUTORS: Authorized to make publication of sales, in certain cases, out of the State, 7.

AGENTS: To distribute fund for relief of soldiers' families at Greenville and Montgomery, Ala., 60. Of the Governor to distribute fund, &c., 40.

ALABAMA & FLORIDA R. R. CO.: Act to amend the charter of, 23.

ANDERSON, WM. E.: An act to extend the provisions of an act for the relief of, 19.

APALACHICOLA CHANNEL COMPANY: Act to incorporate, 12.

APPROPRIATION: An act making appropriations for the expenses of Second Session of the Twelfth General Assembly and for other purposes, 47; Senate, 47; House, 48; Printing and Publishing, 48; general appropriation, 48, 49.

ARSENAL: Joint resolution relative to, 56.

BACON, DR. HENRY: Resolution of thanks to, 52.

BAILEY, WILLIAM: Resolution of thanks to, 52.

BLOCKADE: Resolution in reference to exportation and importation of certain articles by private enterprise, 59.

CATTLE OWNERS: In counties of Levy, Lafayette, Taylor, Wakulla and Duval, act for the protection of, 9.

CAPPLEMAN, D. B., SHERIFF OF MARION COUNTY: Act for the relief of, 25.

CIRCUIT COURT: Judges of may appoint Sheriffs in certain cases, 16; place of holding in Putnam county changed, 8.

CLAIMS: Against State, act providing for the payment of, 22; placed in hands of District Solicitors, 31.

CIVIL AUTHORITY OF THE STATE OF FLORIDA: Resolution relative to, 55.

CLERKS: Of Circuit Courts, fees increased, 22; of Sumter county au_thorized to keep his office at his own house, 30.

CLOTHING: For troops from Florida in Confederate service, 46, 47.

COLUMBIA COUNTY: Boundary line, 11.

CONFISCATED PROPERTY: An act relating to property confiscated to the use of the State, 20; persons having claims against confiscated property, 20; manner of payment of claims, 20; distribution of residue, 21; costs, fees, &c., 21.

COPYING THE LAWS: Resolution in relation to, 58.

COTTON: An act to prevent and punish all persons planting and cultivating over a certain amount of, 42; number of acres that may be planted, 42; penalty, 42; informer, surveyor, 42; hands, 43; manufacturers of, 43; exportation of, 59.

COTTON CARDS: Governor to contract for purchase of, 41.

COURTS: (See Circuit Courts.) Of Probate, an act in relation to holding Probate Courts during the present war, 18.

CRIMINALS: Bonds of, 37.

DISTILLERIES: An act to prevent the distillation of spirituous liquors in the State, 44; Governor to abate distilleries, 44; licenses made void, 44; Governor to issue proclamation, 44; Sheriff refusing to perform duty under this act, 44; contractor with Confederate government, 44 special privilege to Wm. H. Johnson, 45; resolution in relation to, 51'

DaCOSTA, AARON W.: An act for the relief of, 45.

ELECTION LAWS: Relative to soldiers voting, 8, 36, 37.

EXECUTORS: Publication of sales by, may be made out of the State in certain cases, 7.

EXPORTATION: Of certain articles by private enterprise, resolution in reference to, 59.

FASTING, HUMILIATION AND PRAYER: Resolution setting apart a day of, 58.

FLAG: To be furnished to regiments from this State, 46.

FLORIDA, ATLANTIC & GULF CENTRAL R. R. CO.: Act to amend the charter of, 30.

FORFEITED BONDS OF CRIMINALS: 37.

FRAUDS: An act to aid the Confederate Government in the detection of, 35; Judges of Probate to advertise for information, 36; Governor to have evidence recorded, 36.

HOSPITALS: Appropriation for, 41.

HYER, ALBERT: Act for the relief of, 31.

IMPORTATION: Of certain articles by private enterprise, resolution in relation to, 59.

IMPRESSMENT : An act to assist the faithful and necessary enforcement of the impressment act of Congress, &c., 33, 34.

INDIANS: An act to repeal an act entitled an act to regulate trade and intercourse with, 7.

JEFFERSON MANUFACTURING COMPANY: Resolution in relation to exempting the workmen and persons employed in, 59.

JOHNSON, JAMES W.: Act for the relief of 11.

JORDAN, EDWARD, SHERIFF of TAYLOR COUNTY: Act for the relief of, 19.

JUDGES OF PROBATE: Fees increased, 22.

JURORS: Revisal of jury lists, 16; persons in military service, 16.

LANDS: (See Public Lands.)

LOWE, SAMUEL, CLERK OF THE CIRCUIT COURT: An act to legalize the acts of, 38.

McKEOWN, MARGARET J.: Act for the relief of, 25.

MONTICELLO & THOMASVILLE RAIL ROAD: Act to incorporate, 26, 27, 28, 29.

PATROL LAWS: Act to amend, 30.

PENSACOLA, CITY OF: Act amending the charter of, 9, 10, 12.

PERRY, EX-GOV. M. S.: Resolution relative to the accounts of, 57.

PLATS: Furnished the counties of Clay, Jackson and Calhoun, 38.

PROBATE COURTS: An act in relation to holding Probate Courts during the present war, 18.

PUBLIC LANDS: An act to legalize entries of, made after the secession of Florida, and requiring the Receivers to account for the monies received therefor, 17; heirs of soldiers may enter, 49.

RECEIVERS AND REGISTERS, U. S.: Resolution in relation to the accounts of, 57; salaries of, 58.

SALARIES OF PUBLIC OFFICERS: 31.

SHERIFFS: Fees increased, 22.

SOLDIERS: Voting, 8, 36, 37; heirs of may enter certain lands, 49; resolution of thanks to, 51; sick and wounded in Bragg's rmy, 53; of Confederate States, pay of, 58.

SOLDIERS' FAMILIES: An act to provide for the relief of soldiers' families and others that require assistance, 38; appropriation for, 39; persons to be relieved, 39; issue of Treasury notes, 39; list of families, 39; distribution of monies to be made by Governor, 39; Governor may appoint agents, 40; money how to be expended, 40; manner of preparing lists, 40; Governor to advance funds, 40; manner of distribution, 40; cotton cards, 41; County tax, 41; agent for in counties of Santa Rosa and Escambia, 52.

SOLICITOR'S DISTRICT: Act relating to claims placed in the hands of, 31; to be charged with claims, 31; salary may be retained, 32; charges for collections, 32; duty of going out of office, 32.

SPIRITUOUS LIQUORS: (See distilleries,) Act to prevent the distillation of, 44.

STATE BONDS: Destruction of, 54.

STATE OF FLORIDA: Civil authority of, resolution relative to, 55.

SUWANNEE COUNTY: Boundary line of, 11.

TAX ASSESSORS AND COLLECTORS: Act more particularly defining the duties of, 24; times of assessment, 24; tax books, 24.

TAX IN KIND: Resolution relative to, 53.

TOBACCO: (See Cotton.) An act to prevent persons from planting more than a certain amount of, 42.

TREASURY NOTES: Act to provide for an additional issue of, 18; for relief of soldiers' families, 30; Confederate, resolution relative to, 54; State, redeemed, 56.

TREASURER OF THE STATE: Act defining the duties of, 46; salary 21.

WAY SIDE HOMES: Appropriation for, 41.

WAR: Between Confederate States and the United States, resolution in relation to, 60.